The George Foreman Lean Mean Fat Reducing

Grilling Machine Cookbook

THE GEORGE FOREMAN

Lean Mean
Fat Reducing
Grilling Machine
Cookbook

WRITTEN BY

George Foreman & Connie Merydith

Pascoe Publishing
Rocklin, California

Cover design by Salmon Associates
Page design by Melanie Haage Design
Editing by Heidi J. Purvis
Nutritional Analyses by Energy Enterprises

00-102216

ISBN: 1-929862-03-2

00 01 02 03 10 9 8 7 6 5 4 3 2 1

Printed in China

Table of Contents

Dedication

I dedicate this book to my mother, who demonstrated true love for her family every day of the week by the meals she cooked for us. Those meals were simple and sometimes they were lean, but the love she gave in presenting them to us overflows to this day and will always remain.

—George Foreman

For my sons, who are the greatest blessing of my life.

—Connie Merydith

Acknowledgments

We are grateful for the generous assistance of those who helped create this book:

To Jinny Elder, our Nutritionist at Energy Enterprises, who offered expert advice as we created these recipes. She examined and analyzed each recipe and, on many occasions, made suggestions to improve the nutritional value of them.

To our editor, Heidi Jo Purvis, for her attention to the fine details of this book.

And to Terry, Randy, Jessica, Sarah, Jake, Terry H., Lillian and Jason, who enthusiastically tasted and critiqued a wide variety of foods during recipe development.

Dear Friends,

Many of you know me as the heavyweight boxing champion of the world, but very few of you probably know that eating the right kinds of food helped create the foundation for my success and that this remains a key part of my life today.

My story really begins when I was very young. You see, as a kid growing up in Houston, my family didn't always have enough to eat. My mother worked every day of the week to provide for the seven children in our family, but money was scarce and sometimes we were all hungry. I grew up quickly and my appetite was rarely satisfied. My mother could hardly keep up with my constant search for food! But, my mother was very smart and creative in the meals she prepared for us. She would add a small amount of meat to a large amount of vegetables for a main meal. Or, she would dish up vegetables and rice or pasta and leave out the meat altogether. At the time, we didn't realize that we were actually eating a diet that was good for us, we only knew that meat, fish, poultry and specialty foods were pure luxury items. I would save my money whenever I could, a nickel at a time, and use it to buy a big cheeseburger or some other special treat. I was constantly thinking about food! Because of this, you can probably imagine how much I loved steaks, chops, ribs and all the trimmings when I became an adult!

During my boxing career in the 1960s, I was in great physical shape and regularly ate hefty steaks and large

---

> I ate everything I wanted, as often as I wanted . . . I had a heavyweight appetite to match my heavyweight title.

---

green salads as part of my training program. I was a healthy six-foot, four-inch tall boxer and I weighed in around 230 pounds. In those days, when I was hungry—*I was really hungry*! My career as a professional boxer quickly gained momentum and in 1968 I won the heavyweight gold medal for boxing at the Olympics. During the next several years, I ate everything I wanted, as often as I wanted, and by the time I reached

the ultimate status of heavyweight champion of the world, I had a heavyweight appetite to match my heavyweight title.

In 1986, after ten years of retirement from the ring, I sat back and took a hard look at myself. I weighed in at over 300 pounds and was completely out of shape. My diet for the past several years had been whatever I wanted it to be: pizza, fried chicken, ice cream and many fast-food favorites. At the time, I didn't give much thought to the damage those foods were doing to my body. After all, I was retired, right? Wrong. I decided to go back into the boxing ring once again.

To prepare for my introduction back into boxing, I had to look at the types of food I was eating. I was eating large amounts of protein, but not as many carbohydrates as I needed for energy. I was eating a diet very high in fat and I wasn't getting the exercise my body needed for good health. So, I began to run again. I worked on regaining my strength and form. I cut most of the red meat from my diet and concentrated on fish, poultry, complex carbohydrates and other foods that would build up my strength while eliminating the fat. And, when I re-entered the ring in 1987, I was in excellent physical shape and I knew that, once again, I was ready to become a champion.

Today I still enjoy delicious food and I eat with a hearty appetite. But, I choose foods carefully and I watch the amount of fat that I eat. I keep my diet balanced and I exercise regularly to keep myself in good shape. The recipes in this cookbook were created by Connie and myself to help you accomplish exactly the same goals. Inside these chapters you'll find a wide variety of recipes for healthful grilled foods that cut out fat, not the flavor. Each recipe has been analyzed for fat, calories and other important nutritional information. But, just as importantly, these recipes have been created to taste *really* good. Try some of our favorites, such as Orange Pressed Tuna, Jerk Chicken with Cilantro Rice, Creamy Dill Carrots and Quick & Easy Grilled Bananas. A true champion succeeds in reaching the goal he or she desires, whatever that goal may be. We believe that the recipes in this cookbook and the *George Foreman Grilling Machine* can be part of your own success story. Enjoy!

George Foreman

Getting Started with Your George Foreman Lean Mean Fat Reducing Grilling Machine

Grilling is, by far, one of the most popular forms of cooking in the world today. Why? What makes grilling so inviting? When you think of grilling, what comes to mind? A thick, juicy hamburger with all the trimmings? A traditional backyard barbeque for the family? Or, maybe you can almost smell that tantalizing fragrance of smoky barbequed chicken. No matter what you associate with grilling, you'll probably agree with the rest of the world that grilling brings out some of the very best flavors of food.

Why do grilled foods taste *so* good? The process of grilling works by first "searing" the outside of the food and then by "sealing" the juices inside the food. For example, let's imagine a sirloin steak in the grilling process. The steak is placed on the grill and, within a minute or two, the outside is well-browned and slightly charred. That "searing" of the outer edges creates a barrier of sorts that "seals" in the juices of the steak. The inside of the steak remains tender because it is not exposed to the drying source of heat. What's the result? A sirloin steak that is beautifully browned on the outside and deliciously tender and juicy on the inside. Absolute perfection! No wonder grilling has evolved over the years from a simple cooking process to a virtual art form, enjoyed by young and old alike.

In order to grill your favorite foods, you may have considered the many different designs and sizes of grills on the

What is the secret behind the *George Foreman Grilling Machine*?

market. You have probably seen grills advertised for three hundred, five hundred or even several thousand dollars! There are propane grills, charcoal grills and electric grills. There are grills manufactured for your back patio, your stovetop or for the hood of your car (really!). Because grilling has become so incredibly popular there are hundreds of different grills and thousands of tools to accompany them. But, the truth is, the

most versatile and creative grill available today is also one of the easiest to use. We know because we've tested hundreds of recipes and all different types of foods in this incredible grilling machine and it's truly a champion in every sense of the word. We'd like to introduce you to *The George Foreman Lean Mean Fat Reducing Grilling Machine.*

What is the secret behind the *George Foreman Grilling Machine*? Simply this—

■ The unique design of your grilling machine allows fat to drip away from the food as it grills. You'll notice this design as soon as you open the grill. Foods won't sit in fat as they grill. Foods won't absorb grease as they grill. This means that you are able to enjoy your grilled foods without consuming all that fat!

■ The plates of your grilling machine have a special nonstick coating, which means you can now grill your foods without using added butter or oils. You'll taste the full flavor of your favorite foods—without any additional fat! And, when it comes time for clean-up, the nonstick plates make the job quick and easy.

■ The heating elements in your grilling machine cook both sides of your food at once so foods grill faster and more evenly. And, because of this quick grilling process, your foods will retain more natural nutrients.

Your *George Foreman Grilling Machine* offers you the superior flavors of grilled foods and the benefits of healthful cooking—so, let's get started!

GRILLING TIPS

■ Your *George Foreman Grilling Machine* grills at very high temperatures. Use caution when touching the unit as it preheats, grills and cools. If desired, use cooking mitts when you open the grill to baste or season foods during the grilling process.

■ Follow the manufacturer's instructions carefully when using the drip trays, spatulas, and other grilling accessories. The interior of the grill has a special nonstick surface, so use plastic utensils that are heat-tolerant to avoid harming the surface. Avoid using metal forks, knives or tongs.

■ When grilling meats, carefully check for "doneness" by inserting the tip of a sharp knife into the meat. Be careful not to touch the grill with the knife or to completely score through the meat. You may also choose to remove one piece of meat to a board and test it there. Use caution when opening the hot grill at any time.

■ Children may enjoy assisting with food preparation, however they should not touch or use the grill while it is heated. They should not stand near the grill or sit on the kitchen counter as it operates.

■ The drip tray(s) provided with the grill is perfect for catching fat, excess marinades, melted butter, etc. as they drip from foods. Watch the tray carefully as your foods grill to make sure it doesn't overflow and be prepared to use a

---

Find a permanent place on your kitchen counter for your *George Foreman Grilling Machine.*

---

second tray, if necessary. Move the drip tray carefully when it contains hot fat or liquids.

■ Follow the manufacturer's instructions for safely cleaning your grill. Be sure to clean the grill thoroughly and properly each time that you use it. Don't use harsh cleansers or steel scouring pads. Your plastic grilling spatula and a wet sponge

will safely remove any food particles and will protect the nonstick surface of the grill.

■ We recommend that you find a permanent place on your kitchen counter for your *George Foreman Grilling Machine*. Once you've tried a few recipes in the grilling machine and discover how easy it is, we predict that you'll soon be using it every day. So, keep it handy!

SMART EATING FOR HEALTHIER LIVING

Stop for a moment to make a mental list of the foods you've eaten during the past week. Better yet, take a pencil and piece of paper and write it down. You may remember the meals you've eaten, but try to also include the extra sodas, the mid-morning snacks, the popcorn eaten as a late night snack, or the candy purchased from a vending machine. What does your weekly diet look like? Are you comfortable with your food choices? Have you balanced the necessary protein, vegetables, fruits and whole grains during each day? Or, just as so many of us do, would you prefer to move past this subject quickly and forget that you thought about it at all?

The truth is, your body operates best when you make healthful eating choices, but it's all too easy to overlook those choices. Tempting, fat-laden foods are available everywhere—from the grocery store to the gas station and the fast food restaurants in between. With this dilemma, there are two questions to consider: How can you learn to make healthful food choices and, just as important, how can you prepare healthful foods so that you enjoy them just as much (or more) than fatty foods? In this chapter, you'll find some answers to both of these questions. The answers come from what medical and scientific studies tell us and they come from our own personal experiences. So, if you squirmed uncomfortably as you reviewed your weekly diet, take a moment to read this chapter. Start making changes in your diet by trying just one or two of these suggestions this week and add one more each week. At the end of a month, review your eating habits again. We think you'll be surprised by how easy it is to make smart eating choices—one step at a time!

Healthful Food Choices: How to Make Them

Let's answer this question first by examining how our diets became full of fatty foods in the first place. Decades ago, our society formed diets based on the immediate availability of fresh foods. Daily diets consisted of protein foods, grains, flour and cereal, and any fresh fruits and vegetables which were in season and available. Food preservation methods were introduced, but weren't sophisticated. Packaged foods consisted of items that could remain on the shelf for a long time, such as flour, sugar, cornstarch and salt. Most foods containing animal or vegetable fats weren't preserved and had to be consumed soon after they were purchased. In addition to the availability of foods, mealtimes in past decades were also more structured than they are today, simply because meals usually took effort and time to prepare. The "dinner hour" was a leisurely family gathering and the meal, which often took an entire day to prepare, was consumed slowly. So, food choices were based on availability and clearly defined mealtimes.

If we examine our eating patterns today, we can easily see the changes that have been made. Freezing, packaging and food preparation methods now give us a wide array of food choices, available at any time of the day, month or year. The fat in our foods has increased dramatically as we've discovered over the past several years how much the flavor of fat enhances our foods. Take a quick tour of any grocery store and you'll find fresh produce, whole grains and lean cuts of meat. But, you'll also discover crackers, chips and snack items that are loaded with fat. Entire meals, high in fat, are frozen or packaged into boxes to entice diners who don't have time to cook. Deli counters, oriental food departments and bakeries vie for hungry patrons and offer delectable, high-fat selections. Although many of us enjoy the availability of prepared foods, the truth is that most "convenience foods" pack high amounts of fat into our daily diets—and we may not always be aware of it.

Now that we've established how our diets became high in fat, let's think about how to make changes to lower that fat intake. Take the pencil again and sketch out your typical daily eating patterns. Include all your meals, snacks and any special beverages you may drink. With a bit of planning and some "one step at a time" changes, you can significantly change your eating patterns without feeling deprived of your favorite foods. We've listed several suggestions below toward making these changes, but you can also find some through your own creativity. Look at your typical daily meals and select from the following:

- If you enjoy snacking, make one snack a day a "fruit only" snack. Choose any fruit you like. Don't add a high-fat snack to compensate for the fruit snack—simply remove what would be a "typical" snack for you and replace it with a fruit snack.

- If you eat lunch away from home, use your creativity to avoid high-fat meals. When dining in restaurants, choose an entrée that is lighter in fat, such as baked chicken or grilled fish. If a fast food restaurant is your only choice, look for a salad bar, grilled chicken sandwich (without mayonnaise), a child's hamburger or a small taco. Don't be afraid to remove food from your sandwich or off your plate if it is high in fat and you don't want to eat it. Just take it out and eat only what you want. Avoid anything fried or heavily sauced.

- Carry a lowfat granola bar with you AT ALL TIMES. At certain times of the day you are more vulnerable to poor eating choices because of fatigue or hunger. A lowfat granola bar packs well in a purse or briefcase and provides immediate energy. It will also satisfy the craving for something sweet if you are tempted by candy or chocolate. Don't leave home without a lowfat granola bar.

■ Don't try to deny yourself all your favorite foods within a short amount of time. This will only lead to binging because you will feel deprived. Opt instead to slowly remove your high-fat favorites over a period of several weeks or months. Or, you may want to include your favorites at specific planned times. One associate we know eats a very healthful, nutritious diet every day of the month, except for the day that corresponds with his birth date. On that one day of each month, he eats exactly what he wants for his dinner meal, no matter what the fat or calorie content might be. He never feels deprived because he knows that he can look forward to something special on that one day. At the same time, he chooses foods very carefully every other day of the month, so he's established healthful eating patterns.

■ Check the labels at the grocery store. Recent legislation has brought us the best labeling information we've ever had. Use it to check the fat and calorie contents of your favorite foods. Look at the sodium counts and check the percentages of fat in each item. Also, carefully check the serving size for each item. Many serving sizes are smaller than those we might typically eat, so be aware of the suggested serving sizes of foods. Check out healthful snacks such as raisins and other dried fruits, string cheese, pumpkin seeds, rice cakes, turkey jerky, etc. You are not confined to boring snacks when you apply your own creativity and discover the variety of lowfat foods available. Look for lower-fat cuts of beef, poultry and pork and find nonfat dairy items. Check crackers, chips and breads for fat content and make selections accordingly. Your grocery store has never been so well stocked with healthful food choices and the information that accompanies them. Take advantage of it!

- Tell your family and friends that you are making some changes in your diet toward healthier eating patterns. People who care about you will want to support your efforts and will help you avoid some of the more tempting food choices.

- Try to eat proportioned meals every day. Whether you prefer six small meals or three typical meals, make sure that each one is balanced nutritionally. There are no ground rules on the number of meals you must have every day. Busy sched-ules may demand flexibility for you every day of the week. However, you shouldn't allow yourself to become too full or too hungry at any point in a day. Eat what your body needs and sustain it with good choices.

- Try to incorporate 2 to 4 servings of fruit and 3 to 5 servings of vegetables in your diet *every day*. Medical studies clearly show that eating these foods will lower your risk of heart disease, cancer, and other life-threatening diseases, as well as giving your body essential vitamins and minerals necessary

---

You will have more energy, your skin will be healthy and you will notice some significant changes in your waistline, as well!

---

for good health. If that sounds like an overwhelming amount of fruit and vegetables to you, consider that a serving of fruit may be one small can of juice and one serving of vegetables may be one-half cup of green beans.

Start your changes toward healthier living by using these suggestions. Add healthful food selections to your diet as you experiment with foods you like and you'll soon notice that your weekly diet looks quite different from the one you have now. And, just as importantly, your body will begin to reflect the changes in your eating patterns. You will have more energy, your skin will be healthy and you will notice some significant changes in your waistline, as well!

Healthful Food Choices: How to Prepare Them

As important as it is to select healthful foods, it is equally important to prepare them properly. A sure recipe for a diet disaster is to have to eat food that tastes bad. So, how do you prepare foods that are good for you and taste good at the same time? Let's again take a quick look at how our eating patterns have evolved before we answer that question.

In the past several years some fairly standard food preparation techniques were used. Chicken was fried, meatloaf was baked, turkey was roasted and hamburgers were grilled. Steak was broiled, vegetables were boiled and a salad often consisted of fruit embedded in gelatin. Cooking patterns were well established. In recent years, however, we've seen tremendous changes in how our foods are prepared because we've been introduced to a larger world of eating choices and the cooking tools that go with them. We may now use a wok, a steamer, a pasta maker, a rice cooker, a tortilla maker or any other specialty-cooking item. This corresponds to popular recipes that may have their roots in China, India, Thailand or Mexico. With the exciting array of new flavors and spices, we've adapted our cooking preferences to enjoy many of these intercontinental favorites. To fully enjoy the flavors of the lowfat foods we now desire, we offer the following suggestions for food preparation:

■ Foods lose nutrients and texture when overcooked, so cook them only as long as is necessary. One of the reasons we enjoy using the

George Foreman Grilling Machine is that foods grill quickly and retain more nutrients. Some foods, such as poultry and pork, must be completely cooked as a precaution against bacterial contamination, so check for "doneness" just a few minutes prior to the completion of the cooking time. It's always better to check foods a little bit early in the cooking process rather than too late. Some foods, such as fruit, are excellent when cooked, but overcooking will cause them to become mushy. So, again, watch foods closely while cooking to maximize the full flavor and nutrient value of each.

■ Grill or steam vegetables rather than cooking them directly in water. Direct contact with water causes them to lose nutrients. Some vegetables are more flavorful when eaten raw or in salads, so you may want to experiment with leafy green vegetables, squash, broccoli or other vegetables of your choice.

■ Use fresh herbs to enhance the flavor of your foods. In almost any grocery store you'll find fresh basil, rosemary, cilantro, thyme and parsley. These herbs offer delicate flavors that easily complement meats and vegetables. Use them sparingly to avoid overwhelming the natural flavor of your food.

Grill or steam vegetables rather than cooking them directly in water.

■ Choose spices that add personality to your foods. Cumin and chili powder pack a powerful punch that partner well with Southwestern dishes. Lemon pepper enlivens fish and poultry. Salt has many variations, including onion salt, garlic salt, seasoned salt and sea salt, and each has it's own appeal. If your spices are more than a year old, replace them, as the flavors will deteriorate with time.

■ Commercial sauces and marinades work very well with lower-fat meat and poultry choices. Check the fat content and serving size prior to using them. We particularly enjoy Asian chile oil, Szechwan spicy sauce, Teriyaki sauce and flavored vinegars because they offer such bold flavors even when used in small amounts. Lowfat foods become anything but boring when you use some of these exotic sauces!

Use your *George Foreman Grilling Machine* creatively to make up recipes that suit your favorite tastes.

■ Use a small amount of meat in proportion to a larger quantity of carbohydrates or vegetables. For example, use one-half pound of lean hamburger for your favorite pasta sauce instead of the more typical full pound of beef. Use one 8-ounce steak for an Asian noodle salad that will serve 4 people. By stretching the lower amounts of high-fat foods with pasta, rice or vegetables, you will keep the fat content lower and more proportional overall.

■ Use a nonfat cooking spray to coat the surface of your pans. Although the trays of the *George Foreman Grilling Machine* have a nonstick surface, we suggest that you use a nonfat cooking spray for most foods prepared in the grill. This not only helps remove food from the grill, it also helps brown the food. By eliminating oil or butter and using the spray, you're reducing the fat in the foods in a small, but significant way.

■ Use your *George Foreman Grilling Machine* creatively to make up recipes that suit your favorite tastes. Grilling is one of the most healthful ways to prepare foods, so don't be afraid to try recipes that highlight lowfat foods and wonderful flavors. Use the *Basic Cooking Guide* in Chapter 9 as a guide for suggested cooking times of common foods.

■ Lowfat sauces can be just as delicious as the standard high-fat fare. Look for recipes such as the Asparagus with Lemon Dill sauce on page 186 that are used in the *George Foreman Grilling Machine*. Sauces in the grill will heat and melt into the food. The excess sauce will run into the drip tray of the grill. When your food is completely grilled, use the sauce from the drip tray to pour over the individual portions. In this way, you can enjoy the full, delicious flavor of the sauce as it enhances the lowfat food.

A Word About Nutritional Analyses

Each recipe in this cookbook is accompanied by a nutritional analysis that will help you calculate fat, calories, sodium and other helpful information. Use these to select your food choices for each day. The nutritional analyses are based on typical serving sizes and optional ingredients have not been included. When a recipe specifies "lowfat" or "fat-free" ingredients, the nutritional analysis is based on the most common brand of that ingredient.

CHAPTER 2

Bring Out the Best of Grilling—Marinades, Sauces & Rubs

Beef, poultry, pork and fish each have distinctively different flavors and textures. Grilling adds personality to each of these choices, however the addition of a marinade, sauce or rub can make the difference between a standard entrée and a truly memorable one. We don't believe that eating healthy and lowfat food needs to be a boring experience, so we created the following recipes to put a little zip, a bit of a bite and a tiny bit of tanginess into your meals.

Each of these recipes can be made ahead of time and stored, depending on the ingredients in them. Marinades are especially useful when grilling lean cuts of meat because they help break down connective tissue in the meat. Use the marinades when you want to plan ahead for tomorrow or for an evening with guests. To save time, you can prepare marinades in a large, resealable plastic bag and place the meat in it. Close the bag tightly and refrigerate for several hours. When you are ready to grill, simply throw the bag and marinade away. Don't use a marinade as a table sauce unless you boil it for at least 5 minutes first to remove any bacteria.

Try the sauces for a change of pace when you're ready to explore new flavors. Sauces add rich flavor and interest to what can otherwise be a fairly basic cut of poultry or meat. Many sauces are cooked first and used as an accompaniment at the table. To use sauces in your *George Foreman Lean Mean Grilling Machine*, you can either pour one spoonful of sauce over each piece of meat and reserve the rest for the table, or you can

After you've tried these recipes, we hope that you'll experiment with some of your own.

completely cover the meat with sauce. If you choose to cover meat completely with a sauce, the sauce will melt and run into the drip tray, so watch the drip tray carefully and have a second tray handy. If desired, you can use the melted sauce from the drip tray as a table sauce.

Use the rubs when you want to prepare a quick and easy entrée that offers a bold taste. Rubs are a spicy combination of flavors that perk up meat, poultry and fish in a second. As a timesaver, you can mix and store any of these rubs in a resealable plastic bag. When you are ready to grill, you can put the meat into the bag and shake to cover the meat with the spices. Clean up is quick and easy, as you discard the bag and grill the meat. You may also rub meat by putting the spice mixture on a plate and pressing the meat into it.

After you've tried these recipes, we hope that you'll experiment with some of your own. And we've included a Personal Notes section in the back of this cookbook for your own recipes. You'll find that by adding marinades, sauces and rubs to foods that are grilled, you'll make the most of your healthful food choices.

MARINADES

Spicy Orange Marinade

Great with chicken!

½ c.	orange juice
½ t.	orange zest, finely grated
1 t.	Dijon mustard
2 T.	cider vinegar
2 T.	brown sugar
2 T.	olive oil
1	clove garlic, finely chopped

Combine all ingredients in a small saucepan and simmer 3 minutes over low heat. Use immediately or store in an airtight container in the refrigerator for up to 1 week. Makes about ¾ cup.

NUTRITIONAL ANALYSIS: Calories: 25 Total fat: 2 g Saturated fat: >1 g % calories from fat: 64 Carbohydrates: 2 g Protein: 0 g Cholesterol: 0 mg Sodium: 9 mg

Easy Italian Marinade

This "all purpose" marinade is fast to prepare and produces a wonderful flavor.

1	16 oz. bottle fat-free Italian salad dressing
½ t.	black pepper
¼ t.	cayenne pepper
½ t.	dried oregano

Mix all ingredients in a small bowl and pour over beef, chicken or pork. Store any unused marinade in an airtight container in the refrigerator for up to 2 weeks. Makes 2 cups.

NUTRITIONAL ANALYSIS: Calories: 14   Total fat: 0 g   Saturated fat: 0 g
% calories from fat: 0   Carbohydrates: 3 g   Protein: >1 g   Cholesterol: 0 mg   Sodium: 169 mg

Beefy Pepper Marinade

The pepper in this marinade makes the difference!

2 T.	olive oil
¼ c.	white vinegar
½ c.	lemon juice
2 T.	honey
2 t.	black pepper
2	cloves garlic, finely minced

Mix all ingredients in a small bowl to completely dissolve the honey. Use as a marinade for beef or lamb. Store any unused marinade in an airtight container in the refrigerator for up to 1 week. Makes 1 cup.

NUTRITIONAL ANALYSIS: Calories: 8 Total fat: 1g Saturated fat: 1g % calories from fat: 22 Carbohydrates: 3 g Protein: >1 g Cholesterol: 0 mg Sodium: >1 mg

Tangy Pork Marinade

A robust marinade perfect for pork.

2 T.	olive oil
¼ c.	fresh parsley, finely chopped
2	cloves garlic, finely minced
½ t.	black pepper
¼ t.	cayenne pepper
½ c.	Worcestershire sauce
¼ c.	low sodium soy sauce
¼ c.	balsamic vinegar

Combine all ingredients in a small bowl. Store any unused marinade in an airtight container in the refrigerator for up to 1 week. Makes about 1½ cups.

NUTRITIONAL ANALYSIS: Calories: 18 Total fat: 1g Saturated fat: >1g
% calories from fat: 58 Carbohydrates: 2 g Protein: >1 g Cholesterol: 0 mg Sodium: 388 mg

Lemon & Herb Marinade

A light and flavorful marinade.

1 c.	lemon juice
2 T.	olive oil
⅓ c.	red wine vinegar
1 t.	dried oregano
1 t.	dried thyme
1 t.	black pepper
½ t.	salt
1	clove garlic, finely chopped

Mix all ingredients in a small bowl. Store any unused marinade in an air-tight container in the refrigerator for up to 2 weeks. Makes about 1½ cups.

NUTRITIONAL ANALYSIS: Calories: 13   Total fat: 1 g   Saturated fat: >1 g   % calories from fat: 69   Carbohydrates: >1 g   Protein: >1 g   Cholesterol: 0 mg   Sodium: 45 mg

Zesty Beef Marinade

Bold flavors combine for a delightful change!

½ c.	fresh lemon juice
½ c.	balsamic vinegar
½ c.	low sodium soy sauce
2 T.	vegetable oil
¼ c.	Worcestershire sauce
3 T.	fresh parsley, finely minced
3	cloves garlic, finely minced
1 T.	black pepper
1 t.	salt
2 T.	Dijon mustard

Thoroughly combine all ingredients in a small bowl. Store any unused marinade in an airtight container in the refrigerator for up to 1 week. Makes about 2 cups.

NUTRITIONAL ANALYSIS: Calories: 14 Total fat: >1g Saturated fat: >1g % calories from fat: 48 Carbohydrates: 2 g Protein: >1 g Cholesterol: 0 mg Sodium: 313 mg

Herb Mustard Marinade

A marinade that partners well with pork or lamb.

½ c.	Dijon mustard
¼ c.	water
2 T.	olive oil
1 t.	dried thyme
1 t.	dried sage
1 t.	dried rosemary
1	clove garlic, finely minced

Mix all ingredients in a small bowl. Store any unused marinade in an air-tight container in the refrigerator for up to 1 week. Makes about ½ cup.

NUTRITIONAL ANALYSIS: Calories: 26 Total fat: 2 g Saturated fat: >1 g % calories from fat: 77 Carbohydrates: 1 g Protein: >1 g Cholesterol: 0 mg Sodium: 195 mg

East Indian Marinade

Fresh ingredients and flavors make this marinade really special.
Try this with beef, lamb or chicken.

1 t.	fresh mint, finely chopped
¼ t.	salt
1 t.	black pepper
¼ c.	onion, finely chopped
1 T.	fresh parsley, finely chopped
2	cloves garlic, finely minced
1 c.	unflavored, lowfat yogurt
½ c.	cucumber, chopped
½ c.	red tomatoes, chopped

Combine all ingredients in a small bowl. Use immediately. Makes 2 cups.

NUTRITIONAL ANALYSIS: Calories: 7 Total fat: >1 g Saturated fat: >1 g % calories from fat: 18 Carbohydrates: >1 g Protein: >1 g Cholesterol: >1 mg Sodium: 24 mg

Spicy Oriental Marinade

These flavors wake up chicken or beef!

2 T.	peanut oil
1 T.	ground ginger
1 T.	five-spice powder
1 T.	cayenne pepper
½ c.	green onions, finely chopped
½ c.	low sodium soy sauce
¼ c.	red wine vinegar

Mix all ingredients in a small bowl. Store any unused marinade in an air-tight container in the refrigerator for up to 1 week. Makes 1 cup.

NUTRITIONAL ANALYSIS: Calories: 17 Total fat: 1 g Saturated fat: >1 g
% calories from fat: 64 Carbohydrates: 1 g Protein: >1 g Cholesterol: 0 mg Sodium: 374 mg

Greek Island Marinade

Exotic flavor for chicken or lamb!

¼ c.	lemon juice
1 c.	unflavored, lowfat yogurt
½ c.	fresh mint, finely chopped
¼ c.	fresh parsley, finely chopped
¼ c.	onion, finely chopped
½ t.	cayenne pepper
½ t.	black pepper
¼ t.	ground cinnamon

Combine all ingredients in a small bowl. Use immediately. Makes about 2 cups.

NUTRITIONAL ANALYSIS: Calories: 6 Total fat: >1 g Saturated fat: >1 g % calories from fat: 18 Carbohydrates: 1 g Protein: >1 g Cholesterol: >1 mg Sodium: 7 mg

Barbeque Chicken Marinade

This marinade creates a mouth-watering, spicy flavor for chicken or turkey.

1 T.	olive oil
2 t.	salt
6 oz.	tomato paste
1 c.	cider vinegar
2 T.	sugar
1 T.	cayenne pepper
1 c.	nonfat chicken broth
2 T.	Worcestershire sauce

Whisk all ingredients together in a small saucepan and simmer gently for 5 minutes. Refrigerate to cool completely before use. Store in the refrigerator for up to 2 weeks. Makes about 2½ cups.

NUTRITIONAL ANALYSIS: Calories: 9 Total fat: >1g Saturated fat: >1g % calories from fat: 27 Carbohydrates: 2g Protein: >1g Cholesterol: 0mg Sodium: 123mg

Gina's Teriyaki Marinade

A family favorite for flank steak.

¼ c.	vegetable oil
½ c.	low sodium soy sauce
¼ c.	honey
2 T.	vinegar
2 T.	green onions, finely chopped
1½ t.	ground ginger
1	clove garlic, finely minced

Combine all ingredients in a small bowl. Store any unused marinade in an airtight container in the refrigerator for up to 1 week. Makes about 1 cup.

NUTRITIONAL ANALYSIS: Calories: 35   Total fat: 2 g   Saturated fat: >1 g   % calories from fat: 56   Carbohydrates: 4 g   Protein: >1 g   Cholesterol: 0 mg   Sodium: 348 mg

Dill Marinade

This marinade complements fish especially well.

¼ c.	fresh dill, finely minced
1	clove garlic, finely minced
1 c.	unflavored, lowfat yogurt
2 T.	Dijon mustard
2 T.	low sodium soy sauce
1 T.	fresh lemon juice

Mix all ingredients in a small bowl. Use immediately as a marinade for any firm fish. Makes 1½ cups.

NUTRITIONAL ANALYSIS: Calories: 9 Total fat: >1 g Saturated fat: >1 g % calories from fat: 26 Carbohydrates: 1 g Protein: >1 g Cholesterol: >1 mg Sodium: 126 mg

Hot & Spicy Asian Marinade

Asian chile oil and cayenne pepper combine to pack a punch!

2 T.	Asian chile oil
½ t.	cayenne pepper
½ c.	dark brown sugar
1 t.	ground ginger
1 c.	low sodium soy sauce
½ c.	water
½ c.	white vinegar
2	cloves garlic, finely minced

Combine all ingredients in a small bowl. Store any unused marinade in an airtight container in the refrigerator for up to 1 week. Makes about 2½ cups.

NUTRITIONAL ANALYSIS: Calories: 15 Total fat: >1g Saturated fat: >1g % calories from fat: 36 Carbohydrates: 2 g Protein: >1 g Cholesterol: 0 mg Sodium: 346 mg

SAUCES

All American Barbeque Sauce

Everyone's favorite for chicken, ribs, steak and more!

8 oz.	tomato sauce
1	onion, chopped
3	cloves garlic, finely minced
1 T.	fresh parsley, finely minced
1 t.	black pepper
½ t.	cayenne pepper
½ t.	salt
¼ c.	cider vinegar
1 t.	dry yellow mustard

Combine all ingredients in a small saucepan and simmer over low heat for 8–10 minutes. Cool. Use immediately or store in an airtight container in the refrigerator for up to 2 weeks. Makes 1½ cups.

NUTRITIONAL ANALYSIS: Calories: 6 Total fat: >1 g Saturated fat: 0 g % calories from fat: 6 Carbohydrates: 1 g Protein: >1 g Cholesterol: 0 mg Sodium: 66 mg

Beef Rib Sauce

Use as a marinade or dipping sauce for ribs.

4	cloves garlic, finely minced
¼ c.	onion, finely chopped
¼ c.	ketchup
¼ c.	yellow mustard
¼ c.	cider vinegar
¼ c.	water
¼ c.	honey
1 T.	olive oil
1 t.	cayenne pepper

Combine ingredients in a small saucepan. Stir and heat for 5 minutes. Cool. Use immediately or store in an airtight container in the refrigerator for up to 2 weeks. May be frozen, if desired. Makes about 1½ cups.

NUTRITIONAL ANALYSIS: Calories: 19   Total fat: >1 g   Saturated fat: >1 g   % calories from fat: 26   Carbohydrates: 4 g   Protein: >1 g   Cholesterol: 0 mg   Sodium: 54 mg

East West Sauce

A hint of the Orient meets the West.

¼ c.	low sodium soy sauce
½ c.	honey
½ c.	ketchup
1 T.	yellow mustard
1 t.	garlic powder
½ t.	black pepper
½ t.	ground turmeric
1 t.	ground ginger
1 t.	salt

Mix all ingredients in a small saucepan. Simmer over low heat for 5 minutes. Use immediately or store in an airtight container in the refrigerator for up to 2 weeks. Makes 1 cup.

NUTRITIONAL ANALYSIS: Calories: 26 Total fat: >1 g Saturated fat: >1 g % calories from fat: 2 Carbohydrates: 7 g Protein: >1 g Cholesterol: 0 mg Sodium: 289 mg

Southern Barbeque Sauce

A little bit of everything in this yummy sauce!

½ c.	dark brown sugar
2 c.	tomato sauce
¼ c.	cider vinegar
2 T.	yellow mustard
1 t.	cayenne pepper
1 t.	black pepper
2 T.	Worcestershire sauce
¼ t.	paprika
1	clove garlic, finely minced
½	onion, finely chopped

Mix all ingredients thoroughly. Simmer in a medium saucepan over low heat for 10 minutes. Cool. Use immediately or store in an airtight container in the refrigerator for up to 2 weeks. Makes about 2½ cups.

NUTRITIONAL ANALYSIS: Calories: 12 Total fat: >1 g Saturated fat: >1 g
% calories from fat: 4 Carbohydrates: 3 g Protein: >1 g Cholesterol: 0 mg Sodium: >1 mg

Butter & Herb Sauce

The sweet herbs in this sauce accompany poultry very well.

½ c.	lowfat butter
½ t.	lemon zest
2 T.	fresh lemon juice
1 T.	fresh parsley, finely minced
1 t.	basil
1 t.	thyme
1 t.	sage

Whisk all ingredients in a small bowl. Brush on chicken or turkey before grilling. Makes ½ cup.

NUTRITIONAL ANALYSIS: Calories: 71 Total fat: 8 g Saturated fat: 2 g
% calories from fat: 97 Carbohydrates: >1 g Protein: >1 g Cholesterol: 0 mg Sodium: 78 mg

Steak Dipping Sauce

This full-bodied sauce provides plenty of flavor for any cut of beef.

8 oz.	tomato sauce
2 T.	yellow mustard
2 T.	dark brown sugar
2 T.	low sodium soy sauce
2 T.	cider vinegar
2 T.	Worcestershire sauce
1 T.	lemon juice
2	cloves garlic, finely minced
1	small onion, finely chopped
1 T.	fresh parsley, finely minced

Combine all ingredients in a small saucepan and simmer over low heat for about 15 minutes. Sauce should be thickened slightly when done. Cool.

Use immediately or store in an airtight container in the refrigerator for up to 2 weeks. Makes 1½ cups.

NUTRITIONAL ANALYSIS: Calories: 8 Total fat: >1 g Saturated fat: 0 g % calories from fat: 6 Carbohydrates: 2 g Protein: >1 g Cholesterol: 0 mg Sodium: 112 mg

Sweet Cranberry Sauce

The perfect sauce to accompany grilled turkey breast.

½ c.	onion, finely chopped
2 T.	cider vinegar
¼ c.	dark molasses
1 c.	cranberry juice
8 oz.	tomato sauce

Combine all ingredients in a small saucepan and simmer for 10 minutes. Do not allow the sauce to boil. Serve warm with poultry. Makes 2½ cups.

NUTRITIONAL ANALYSIS: Calories: 12 Total fat: >1 g Saturated fat: 0 g % calories from fat: 1 Carbohydrates: 3 g Protein: >1 g Cholesterol: 0 mg Sodium: 4 mg

Quick & Easy Oriental Sauce

A super-fast spicy sauce for any night of the week.

½ c.	hoisin sauce
½ c.	low sodium soy sauce
1 t.	Asian chile oil

Mix all the ingredients in a small saucepan and heat until warm, but not boiling. Simmer for 3 minutes to combine flavors. Serve warm. Makes 1 cup.

NUTRITIONAL ANALYSIS: Calories: 18 Total fat: >1 g Saturated fat: 0 g % calories from fat: 16 Carbohydrates: 3 g Protein: >1 g Cholesterol: 0 mg Sodium: 510 mg

Honey Mustard Dipping Sauce

Favorite flavors combine in this lowfat sauce.

½ c.	yellow mustard
2 T.	cider vinegar
2	cloves garlic, finely minced
¼ c.	honey
1 t.	lemon juice
½ t.	cayenne pepper
1 T.	lowfat butter

Combine all the ingredients in a small saucepan. Heat for 4 minutes, or until the honey is completely dissolved and the sauce is slightly thickened. Serve warm. Makes ¾ cup.

NUTRITIONAL ANALYSIS: Calories: 24 Total fat: >1 g Saturated fat: >1 g % calories from fat: 29 Carbohydrates: 4 g Protein: >1 g Cholesterol: 0 mg Sodium: 88 mg

Sweet & Sour Sauce

Brush this sauce over grilled chicken, pork or vegetables for excellent flavor.

1 T.	cornstarch
1 T.	water
1 T.	low sodium soy sauce
½ c.	nonfat chicken broth
¼ c.	cider vinegar
2 T.	clover honey
2 T.	lemon juice
2 T.	tomato paste

Combine the cornstarch and water in a small bowl. Set aside. In a small saucepan, combine the remaining ingredients. Heat and stir until bubbling. Slowly add the cornstarch-water mixture to the sauce. Simmer and stir for 3 minutes. The sauce will be thickened and smooth when done. Serve warm. Makes 1 cup.

NUTRITIONAL ANALYSIS: Calories: 10 Total fat: 0 g Saturated fat: 0 g
% calories from fat: 0 Carbohydrates: 2 g Protein: >1 g Cholesterol: 0 mg Sodium: 49 mg

Mango Tomato Salsa

Tart and sweet!

2 c.	mangos, chopped
3	ripe tomatoes, chopped
½ c.	purple onion, finely chopped
2 T.	fresh cilantro, finely minced
2	cloves garlic, finely minced
1 T.	olive oil
1 T.	lemon juice
1 T.	lime juice
½ t.	black pepper
½ t.	salt

Lightly mix all ingredients in a medium-sized serving bowl. Chill to serve. Makes about 3 cups.

NUTRITIONAL ANALYSIS: Calories: 8 Total fat: >1 g Saturated fat: 0 g % calories from fat: 28 Carbohydrates: 1 g Protein: >1 g Cholesterol: 0 mg Sodium: 20 mg

Peach & Papaya Salsa

A colorful citrus complement for poultry or fish.

2 c.	peaches, chopped
2 c.	papayas, chopped
2 T.	honey
2 T.	lemon juice
2 T.	purple onion, finely chopped
2 T.	fresh cilantro, finely minced
½ t.	black pepper
½ t.	salt

Combine all the ingredients in a medium-sized serving bowl. Chill to serve. Makes 4 cups salsa.

NUTRITIONAL ANALYSIS: Calories: 7 Total fat: 0 g Saturated fat: >1 g
% calories from fat: 2 Carbohydrates: 2 g Protein: >1 g Cholesterol: 0 mg Sodium: 20 mg

RUBS

Heavy Duty Garlic Rub

Best with beef.

10	cloves garlic, finely minced
1 t.	ketchup
1 t.	cracked black pepper
½ t.	salt
1 T.	olive oil

Mix all ingredients to make a thick paste. Generously press into all sides of the beef. Use immediately. Makes enough for 1 large or 2 small steaks.

NUTRITIONAL ANALYSIS: Calories: 46   Total fat: 4 g   Saturated fat: >1 g   % calories from fat: 67   Carbohydrates: 3 g   Protein: >1 g   Cholesterol: 0 mg   Sodium: 320 mg

Spicy Chicago Rub

For pork, beef or chicken.

1 T.	black pepper
¼ c.	paprika
1 T.	salt
2 T.	chili powder
1 T.	onion powder
1 T.	garlic powder
1 T.	dried parsley
⅓ c.	brown sugar

Combine all ingredients in a small bowl. Mix thoroughly with a fork to evenly distribute the sugar. Store in an airtight container in the refrigerator for up to 3 months. Makes ¾ cup.

NUTRITIONAL ANALYSIS: Calories: 42 Total fat: >1 g Saturated fat: >1 g % calories from fat: 11 Carbohydrates: 10 g Protein: >1 g Cholesterol: 0 mg Sodium: 642 mg

Southern Onion Rub

Dehydrated onions give this rub an exciting flavor!

2 T.	dehydrated minced onions
¼ c.	paprika
1 T.	black pepper
2 t.	cayenne pepper
2 t.	onion powder
1 t.	salt

Combine all ingredients in a small bowl. Store in an airtight container in the refrigerator for up to 3 months. Makes ½ cup.

NUTRITIONAL ANALYSIS: Calories: 27 Total fat: 1 g Saturated fat: >1 g % calories from fat: 25 Carbohydrates: 7 g Protein: 2 g Cholesterol: 0 mg Sodium: 321 mg

Chicken Paprika Rub

This rub gives grilled chicken a beautiful color and spicy taste.

½ c.	paprika
1 T.	dried parsley
2 T.	onion powder
1 T.	cayenne pepper
2 t.	black pepper, coarsely ground
1 t.	salt

Combine all ingredients in a small bowl. Store in an airtight container in the refrigerator for up to 3 months. Makes ½ cup.

NUTRITIONAL ANALYSIS: Calories: 33 Total fat: 1 g Saturated fat: >1 g % calories from fat: 25 Carbohydrates: 7 g Protein: 2 g Cholesterol: 0 mg Sodium: 320 mg

Southwest Rub

Flavors that capture the West and Mexico.

½ t.	ground cumin
½ t.	ground cinnamon
½ t.	ground coriander
1 t.	paprika
1 t.	chili powder
½ t.	cayenne pepper
1 T.	black pepper
1 T.	garlic salt

Combine all ingredients in a small bowl. Store in an airtight container in the refrigerator for up to 3 months. Makes ½ cup.

NUTRITIONAL ANALYSIS: Calories: 24 Total fat: >1 g Saturated fat: >1 g
% calories from fat: 21 Carbohydrates: 5 g Protein: 1 g Cholesterol: 0 mg Sodium: 236 mg

Three Alarm Rub

This hot, hot, hot rub is great with beef and lamb.

1 T.	cayenne pepper
2 T.	black pepper
2 T.	chili powder
2 T.	onion powder
2 T.	garlic powder
1 T.	salt
1 T.	sugar
¼ c.	paprika

Combine all ingredients in a small bowl. Store in an airtight container in the refrigerator for up to 3 months. Makes ¾ cup.

NUTRITIONAL ANALYSIS: Calories: 38 Total fat: >1 g Saturated fat: >1 g % calories from fat: 17 Carbohydrates: 8 g Protein: 1 g Cholesterol: 0 mg Sodium: 827 mg

Italian Pork Rub

Perfect for pork chops!

½ t.	black pepper
½ t.	cayenne pepper
¼ c.	paprika
2 t.	dried oregano
2 t.	garlic powder
2 t.	onion powder
2 t.	Italian seasoning
1 t.	salt

Combine all ingredients in a small bowl. Store in an airtight container in the refrigerator for up to 3 months. Makes ¼ cup.

NUTRITIONAL ANALYSIS: Calories: 34 Total fat: >1 g Saturated fat: >1 g % calories from fat: 21 Carbohydrates: 7 g Protein: 1 g Cholesterol: 0 mg Sodium: 572 mg

Mustard Pepper Rub

Great with pork or beef.

1 T.	dry mustard
¼ c.	paprika
2 T.	black pepper
1 T.	cayenne pepper
1 T.	sugar

Combine all ingredients in a small bowl. Store in an airtight container in the refrigerator for up to 3 months. Makes ½ cup.

NUTRITIONAL ANALYSIS: Calories: 47   Total fat: 2 g   Saturated fat: >1 g   % calories from fat: 27   Carbohydrates: 9 g   Protein: 2 g   Cholesterol: 0 mg   Sodium: 4 mg

Savory Spice Rub

A lovely blend of spices to accompany grilled vegetables.

1 T.	black pepper
2 t.	cayenne pepper
1 t.	dried oregano
1 t.	dried basil
1 T.	paprika
2 T.	light brown sugar
1 T.	salt
2 t.	garlic powder
2 t.	onion powder
1 T.	chili powder

Combine all ingredients in a small bowl. Store in an airtight container in the refrigerator for up to 3 months. Makes ½ cup.

NUTRITIONAL ANALYSIS: Calories: 35 Total fat: >1 g Saturated fat: >1 g
% calories from fat: 14 Carbohydrates: 8 g Protein: >1 g Cholesterol: 0 mg Sodium: 1,348 mg

Lemon Pepper Rub

Partners beautifully with fish and poultry.

2 t.	lemon pepper
1 t.	lemon juice
2 t.	fresh rosemary, minced
1 T.	fresh dill, finely minced
1 t.	salt
1 t.	black pepper
2	cloves garlic, finely minced

Combine all ingredients in a small bowl. Use immediately as a rub for fish or poultry. Discard leftovers. Makes ¼ cup.

NUTRITIONAL ANALYSIS: Calories: 15 Total fat: >1 g Saturated fat: >1 g % calories from fat: 14 Carbohydrates: 3 g Protein: >1 g Cholesterol: 0 mg Sodium: 1,752 mg

CHAPTER 3

A Cut Above—Beef & Lamb

Beef is one of the world's most highly prized meats and, with a pleasing texture and generous flavor, beef has always been a popular choice for the grill. However, beef is also known as a higher-fat food choice, so we have created recipes in this chapter using some cuts of beef that offer the rich flavor you want with less fat than you would imagine. Tenderloin, flank steak, London broil, top and bottom round steak and lean hamburger are some of the beef cuts that make sense when you're looking for lower-fat beef choices.

In addition to purchasing lower-fat cuts of beef, you may want to consider smaller portions of beef. Beef has traditionally been served in 8–12 ounce portions, however, by reducing portions to 4–6 ounces, you can significantly lower the fat while enjoying the flavor of beef. Also, some preparation methods for beef help make the most of the lower-fat cuts. For example, some recipes in this cookbook direct you to slice the beef thinly across the grain of the meat to serve. Slicing the beef in this manner helps make a lean cut of beef more palatable and tender as it's eaten.

We've included recipes using lamb in this chapter because it can also be a healthy choice when served in small portions. Lamb is very rich meat and it grills well in the *George Foreman Grilling Machine*. We've paired lamb with vegetables and fruit and used spices and herbs to complement the food combinations. Herbs such as rosemary and certain flavors such as mint are excellent companions to lamb.

There is no need to turn over any cut of meat . . . the grill cooks both sides at once.

To ensure that the grilled beef and lamb do not overcook, check the meat a few minutes before it should be done. It's easy to continue grilling meat that is too rare, but impossible to correct overcooked meat. If the meat is not the same thickness throughout the entire cut, you may find that part of the meat shows grill "char marks" and another part may not. You may turn the meat around to "even" these marks, if you desire, but the marks will not affect the flavor or result of the grilled meat. Use a heat-tolerant plastic fork or the plastic grilling spatula whenever you choose to reposition meat. Also, you may find that, if you have several cuts of meat in the grill, some pieces may grill more quickly than others. If this occurs, you may simply reposition the meat in the grill, or you can remove some portions and allow others to grill for an extra minute or so. It is probable that each member of your family has different preferences regarding the "doneness" of the meat, so you may want to position the meat to remove some cuts when rare and others when well-done. There is no need to turn over any cut of meat because the grill cooks both sides of the meat at the same time.

To make kebabs, use wooden skewers only and we recommend that you soak them first in water for about 20 minutes. Drain them and use them as directed in these recipes for the *George Foreman Grilling Machine*. Soaking the skewers in water first allows food to slide more easily on and off the skewers and also keeps them from burning in the grill as the food cooks.

BEEF STEAKS & CUTS

Mushroom Tenderloin Steaks

A tasty entrée for a busy weeknight.

4	4 oz. tenderloin steaks
1 T.	parsley, finely minced
1	clove garlic, finely minced
1 t.	salt
½ t.	black pepper
4 oz.	canned mushroom slices, drained
	nonfat cooking spray

Coat the grill with cooking spray and preheat for 5 minutes. Remove any visible fat from the steaks. Place the steaks in the grill and sprinkle with the parsley, garlic, salt and pepper. Grill for 4 minutes. Spoon the mushroom slices over the steaks and grill for an additional 1–2 minutes. Serves 4.

NUTRITIONAL ANALYSIS: Calories: 145 Total fat: 5 g Saturated fat: 2 g % calories from fat: 33 Carbohydrates: 2 g Protein: 22 g Cholesterol: 62 mg Sodium: 750 mg

Southwestern Rubbed Steak

Use spices generously to make this steak special!

1 lb.	tenderloin steak
1 t.	salt
1 T.	brown sugar
½ t.	cumin
1 t.	chili powder
½ t.	cayenne pepper
	nonfat cooking spray

Remove any visible fat from the steak. Mix together the salt, sugar, cumin, chili powder and cayenne pepper. Press the spices firmly onto all sides of the steak and let stand for 5 minutes. Lightly coat the grill with cooking spray and preheat for 5 minutes. Grill the steak for 5–7 minutes, or according to your preference. Cut the steak into 4 portions or slice thinly and serve on a warm platter. Serves 4.

NUTRITIONAL ANALYSIS: Calories: 148   Total fat: 5 g   Saturated fat: 2 g   % calories from fat: 33   Carbohydrates: 3 g   Protein: 21 g   Cholesterol: 62 mg   Sodium: 635 mg

Spicy Pepper Steak

Accompany this steak with angel hair pasta and a fresh green salad and dinner is done!

1 lb.	bottom round steak
1 t.	salt
½ t.	pepper
¼ t.	cayenne pepper
1	green pepper, seeded and sliced into thin rings
1	red pepper, seeded and sliced into thin rings
1	onion, sliced into thin rings
	nonfat cooking spray

Coat the grill with cooking spray and preheat for 5 minutes. Remove any visible fat from the steak and cut diagonally across the grain into thin slices. Place the steak slices in the grill and sprinkle with the salt, pepper and cayenne pepper. Grill for 2 minutes. Add the green and red pepper and the onion slices. Grill for 3–5 minutes, or until the vegetables are tender-crisp. Serves 4.

NUTRITIONAL ANALYSIS: Calories: 183   Total fat: 7 g   Saturated fat: 3 g   % calories from fat: 34   Carbohydrates: 7 g   Protein: 23 g   Cholesterol: 66 mg   Sodium: 619 mg

Grilled Asian Beef

Marinate these steaks for full flavor!

4	6 oz. ribeye steaks
½ c.	low sodium soy sauce
2	cloves garlic, finely minced
1 T.	vegetable oil
1 T.	white vinegar
1 T.	brown sugar
1 t.	ground ginger
	nonfat cooking spray

Remove any visible fat from the steaks and place in a flat glass pan. Combine the soy sauce, garlic, oil, vinegar, sugar and ginger in a small bowl and mix well. Pour over the steaks and marinate for at least 1 hour. Spray the grill with the cooking spray and preheat for 5 minutes. Grill the steaks for 5–7 minutes, or according to your preference. Serves 4.

NUTRITIONAL ANALYSIS: Calories: 207 Total fat: 9 g Saturated fat: 4 g
% calories from fat: 43 Carbohydrates: 6 g Protein: 20 g Cholesterol: 52 mg Sodium: 1,113 mg

Onion Butter London Broil

For best results, grill until the beef is rare or medium-rare.

1½ lb.	London broil steak, 1½-inch thick
½ c.	lowfat margarine
1 t.	Worcestershire sauce
1	clove garlic, finely minced
2 T.	parsley, finely minced
2 T.	green onions, finely chopped
	nonfat cooking spray

Coat the grill with cooking spray and preheat for 5 minutes. In a small bowl, combine the margarine and Worcestershire sauce. Blend well. Add the garlic, parsley and green onions. Remove any visible fat from the steak and grill the steak for 3 minutes. Brush the butter-herb sauce over the steak and grill for an additional 4–5 minutes. As the butter sauce melts, it will run into the drip tray. To serve, slice thinly across the grain and arrange on a warm platter. Pour the melted butter sauce from the drip tray over the sliced beef. Serves 6.

NUTRITIONAL ANALYSIS: Calories: 217   Total fat: 13 g   Saturated fat: 5 g
% calories from fat: 59   Carbohydrates: 1 g   Protein: 18 g   Cholesterol: 52 mg   Sodium: 156 mg

Sunday Beef Kebabs

Tender beef combines with fresh vegetables and a touch of Oriental sauce.

1 lb.	beef sirloin
1 c.	fresh or canned pineapple chunks
8	cherry tomatoes
1	green pepper, cut into 1-inch pieces
8	mushrooms
¼ c.	low sodium soy sauce
2 T.	honey
½ t.	ground ginger
1 T.	garlic, finely minced
8	10-inch wooden skewers, soaked in water and drained
	nonfat cooking spray

Remove any visible fat from the beef and cut into 1-inch cubes. Coat the grill with cooking spray and preheat for 5 minutes. Thread the meat onto 4 skewers. Thread the pineapple, tomatoes, green pepper and mushrooms onto 4 skewers, alternating each. In a small bowl, mix the soy sauce, honey, ginger and garlic. Brush the sauce over the beef and the vegetables. Place the beef skewers in the grill widthwise (horizontally) and cook for 5 minutes. Add the vegetable skewers widthwise and grill for an additional 3–4 minutes. Serves 4.

NUTRITIONAL ANALYSIS: Calories: 226   Total fat: 5 g   Saturated fat: 2 g   % calories from fat: 19   Carbohydrates: 20 g   Protein: 26 g   Cholesterol: 68 mg   Sodium: 610 mg

Milano Sirloin Steaks

A little touch of Italy!

1 lb.	sirloin steaks
2 T.	fresh basil, finely minced
½ t.	dried oregano
1 t.	black pepper
½ t.	salt
2 c.	red tomatoes, coarsely chopped
	nonfat cooking spray

Coat the grill with cooking spray and preheat for 5 minutes. Remove any visible fat from the steaks. Place the steaks in the grill and sprinkle with the basil, oregano, pepper and salt. Grill for 5 minutes. Add the tomatoes and grill for 2–4 minutes. As the tomatoes grill, the juice will collect in the drip tray. If desired, you may pour the juice over the grilled steaks to serve. Serves 4.

NUTRITIONAL ANALYSIS: Calories: 157   Total fat: 5 g   Saturated fat: 2 g
% calories from fat: 31   Carbohydrates: 5 g   Protein: 22 g   Cholesterol: 62 mg   Sodium: 345 mg

Dijon Flank Steak

Grill with Vidalia onions for a perfect dinner.

1½ lb.	flank steak
1 T.	Dijon mustard
¼ c.	cider vinegar
1 t.	salt
½ t.	black pepper
1	Vidalia onion, thinly sliced
	nonfat cooking spray

Remove any visible fat from the steak and place the steak in a flat glass pan. In a small bowl, combine the mustard, vinegar, salt and pepper and pour over the steak. Refrigerate, covered, for 30 minutes. Coat the grill with cooking spray and preheat for 5 minutes. Grill the steak for 4 minutes. Add the sliced onions and continue grilling for 3–4 minutes. Slice the beef thinly across the grain and serve topped with the onions. Serves 6.

NUTRITIONAL ANALYSIS: Calories: 180 Total fat: 8 g Saturated fat: 4 g
% calories from fat: 43 Carbohydrates: 3 g Protein: 22 g Cholesterol: 54 mg Sodium: 519 mg

Hawaiian Pineapple Beef

Flavorful and delicious!

1½ lb.	London broil steak
2 T.	green onion, finely minced
1 t.	ground ginger
1 T.	honey
½ c.	fresh pineapple, cut into small pieces (or ½ c. canned pineapple chunks, drained) nonfat cooking spray

Lightly coat the grill with cooking spray and preheat for 5 minutes. Remove any visible fat from the steak and grill the steak for 2 minutes. In a small bowl, combine the green onion, ginger, honey and mix well. Spoon the sauce over the steak and grill for 3 minutes. Add the pineapple pieces on top of and around the steak and grill for 2–4 minutes. To serve, slice the steak thinly across the grain and serve with the warm pineapple. Serves 6.

NUTRITIONAL ANALYSIS: Calories: 193 Total fat: 6 g Saturated fat: 4 g
% calories from fat: 33 Carbohydrates: 5 g Protein: 23 g Cholesterol: 65 mg Sodium: 70 mg

Stuffed Steak Olé

A delectable combination of grilled beef and fresh vegetable salsa.

2 lbs.	flank steak
2 c.	fresh tomato, chopped
¼ c.	fresh cilantro, finely minced
2	cloves garlic, finely minced
½ c.	onion, chopped
¼ c.	green pepper, chopped
½ t.	cumin
½ t.	cayenne pepper
½ t.	salt
	nonfat cooking spray

Remove any visible fat from the steak. With a sharp knife, cut a slit sideways into the steak to create a pocket, without cutting completely through the meat. In a medium bowl, combine the tomato, cilantro, garlic, onion, green pepper, cumin, pepper and salt. Mix well and stuff the pocket of the steak with the vegetable-herb salsa. Press the sides of the steak to close or secure with toothpicks, if desired. Coat the grill with cooking spray and preheat for 5 minutes. Grill the stuffed steak for 9–11 minutes, or according to your taste. To serve, cut the steak across the grain into ¼-inch slices. Top the slices with any remaining vegetable-herb salsa. Serves 6.

NUTRITIONAL ANALYSIS: Calories: 262 Total fat: 12 g Saturated fat: 5 g
% calories from fat: 42 Carbohydrates: 5 g Protein: 32 g Cholesterol: 78 mg Sodium: 298 mg

T-bone Steaks with Barbeque Butter

*T-bone steaks are juicy and delicious, but they can also be
very high in fat. To control that fat, use a sharp knife to remove
as much visible fat as possible and keep portions small.*

4	6 oz. T-bone steaks
2 T.	Worcestershire sauce
¼ c.	lowfat margarine
¼ c.	green onions, chopped
1 t.	salt
¼ t.	black pepper

Remove any visible fat from the steaks. Preheat the grill for 5 minutes. In a small bowl, combine the Worcestershire sauce, margarine, green onions, salt and pepper. Place the steaks in the grill and cover each with the barbeque butter. Grill the steaks for 8–9 minutes, or according to your preference. As the butter melts, it will run into the drip tray. Serves 4.

NUTRITIONAL ANALYSIS: Calories: 208 Total fat: 10 g Saturated fat: 4 g
% calories from fat: 47 Carbohydrates: 3 g Protein: 23 g Cholesterol: 65 mg Sodium: 796 mg

Teriyaki Beef

Serve over steamed rice for a traditional delight.

1 lb.	lean beef (such as flank steak, or bottom round)
¼ c.	sesame oil
¼ c.	low sodium soy sauce
¼ c.	cider vinegar
2 T.	honey
2 T.	green onion, chopped
2	cloves garlic, chopped
1 t.	ginger
	nonfat cooking spray

Remove any visible fat from the beef and place the steak in a flat glass pan. Combine the oil, soy sauce, vinegar, honey, green onion, garlic and ginger and pour over the meat. Cover tightly and marinate in the refrigerator for 2–12 hours. Coat the grill with cooking spray and preheat for 5 minutes. Grill the beef for 6–7 minutes, or according to your preference. Slice thinly across the grain of the beef. If you choose to use the marinade as a sauce, boil it for at least 5 minutes before serving. Serves 4.

NUTRITIONAL ANALYSIS: Calories: 359 Total fat: 23 g Saturated fat: 6 g
% calories from fat: 56 Carbohydrates: 14 g Protein: 26 g Cholesterol: 59 mg Sodium: 1,065 mg

Mediterranean Beef & Vegetable Grill

Tempting and lowfat!

1 lb.	flank steak
1	small zucchini, cut into 1-inch cubes
1	small tomato, cut into 8 pieces
¼	onion, cut into ¼-inch pieces
1	green pepper, cut into ¼-inch pieces
1 T.	balsamic vinegar
1 t.	black pepper, coarsely ground
1 t.	garlic salt
8	10-inch wooden skewers, soaked in water and drained
	nonfat cooking spray

Partially freeze the flank steak (for about 30 minutes). Remove any visible fat and cut the beef into very thin slices across the grain of the meat. Thread the steak through 4 of the skewers in an accordion fashion. Set aside. Thread the vegetables through the remaining 4 skewers, alternating vegetables on each. In a small bowl, mix together the vinegar, pepper and garlic salt. Lightly coat the grill with cooking spray and preheat for 5 minutes. Place the beef skewers in the grill widthwise (horizontally) and grill for 4 minutes. Add the vegetable skewers (widthwise) and sprinkle all the skewers with the vinegar, pepper and garlic salt mixture. Grill for an additional 3–4 minutes. Serves 4.

NUTRITIONAL ANALYSIS: Calories: 203 Total fat: 9g Saturated fat: 4g
% calories from fat: 40 Carbohydrates: 5 g Protein: 25 g Cholesterol: 59 mg Sodium: 530 mg

Pepper Crusted Steak

The rich flavor of steak mingles with a spicy pepper crust.

1 lb.	flank steak
2 T.	black pepper, coarsely ground
1 t.	seasoned salt
1 t.	garlic powder
1 T.	fresh parsley, finely minced
	nonfat cooking spray

Remove any visible fat from the steak. Combine the pepper, salt, garlic powder and parsley and press firmly into all sides of the steak. Coat the grill with cooking spray and preheat for 5 minutes. Grill the steak for 7–8 minutes, or according to your preference. To serve, slice thinly across the grain. Serves 4.

NUTRITIONAL ANALYSIS: Calories: 192   Total fat: 9 g   Saturated fat: 4 g
% calories from fat: 43   Carbohydrates: 3 g   Protein: 24 g   Cholesterol: 59 mg   Sodium: 422 mg

Lime Steak Fajitas

In the true style of Mexico, a bit of tender meat is added to fresh vegetables and toppings to create a memorable meal.

½ lb.	flank steak
⅓ c.	lime juice
1 t.	black pepper
½ t.	cayenne pepper
1	green pepper
1	red pepper
1	small white onion
8	flour tortillas, warmed
½ c.	lowfat cheddar cheese, shredded
½ c.	lowfat sour cream
	nonfat cooking spray

Remove any visible fat from the steak. Cut the steak into very thin slices and place in a flat glass pan. Mix together the lime juice and black pepper and pour over the steak. Refrigerate for 2–4 hours. Remove the seeds and inner fibers from the green and red peppers and cut into very thin slices. Cut the onion into thin slices and separate the rings. Coat the grill with cooking spray and preheat for 5 minutes. Grill the steak for 3 minutes. Add the peppers and onion on top of the steak and grill for 4–5 minutes. To serve, fill tortillas with the meat and vegetables and pass the cheese and sour cream to add as desired. Serves 8.

NUTRITIONAL ANALYSIS: Calories: 254 Total fat: 8 g Saturated fat: 3 g
% calories from fat: 27 Carbohydrates: 32 g Protein: 14 g Cholesterol: 21 mg Sodium: 314 mg

BEEF RIBS

Oriental Beef Short Ribs

Tender and juicy!

3 lbs.	beef short ribs
1	clove garlic, finely chopped
½ c.	low sodium soy sauce
1 t.	sesame oil
1 t.	ground ginger
2 T.	honey
1 T.	cider vinegar
	nonfat cooking spray

Parboil the ribs for 20 minutes. (To parboil ribs: cook the ribs for 20 minutes in a steamer rack over a pan of boiling water). Cool and remove any visible fat. Place the ribs in a flat glass pan. In a small bowl, blend the garlic, soy sauce, oil, ginger, honey and vinegar until the honey is dissolved. Pour the marinade over the ribs, cover the pan tightly and refrigerate for 2–12 hours. Lightly coat the grill with cooking spray and preheat for 5 minutes. Grill the ribs for 8–9 minutes, or until the ribs are lightly charred and the meat is completely cooked. Serves 4.

NUTRITIONAL ANALYSIS: Calories: 295 Total fat: 14 g Saturated fat: 7 g
% calories from fat: 44 Carbohydrates: 12 g Protein: 29 g Cholesterol: 82 mg Sodium: 1,118 mg

Classic BBQ Beef Ribs

A family favorite—without all the fat!

5 lbs.	beef loin ribs (12–15 ribs)
½ c.	ketchup
2 T.	prepared mustard
1 T.	Worcestershire sauce
1	clove garlic, finely minced
1 T.	brown sugar
	nonfat cooking spray

Parboil the ribs for 20 minutes. (To parboil ribs: cook the ribs for 20 minutes in a steamer rack over a pan of boiling water). Cool and remove any visible fat from the ribs. Coat the grill with cooking spray and preheat for 5 minutes. In a small bowl, combine the ketchup, mustard, Worcestershire sauce, garlic and brown sugar. Grill the ribs for 3 minutes and baste with the sauce. Grill for an additional 2 minutes and baste again, turning the ribs to coat thoroughly. Grill 2 minutes. Serve the ribs with any remaining sauce. Serves 6.

NUTRITIONAL ANALYSIS: Calories: 518 Total fat: 29 g Saturated fat: 15 g
% calories from fat: 51 Carbohydrates: 8 g Protein: 55 g Cholesterol: 181 mg Sodium: 475 mg

LAMB CHOPS

Dijon Citrus Lamb Chops

Orange and mustard flavors accent these tender chops.

4	4–6 oz. lamb loin chops
¼ c.	Dijon mustard
1 T.	orange juice
1 t.	brown sugar
½ t.	black pepper
¼ t.	salt
2	oranges, peeled and cut into ½-inch rings
	nonfat cooking spray

Remove any visible fat from the lamb chops. Lightly coat the grill with cooking spray and preheat for 5 minutes. In a small bowl, blend the mustard, juice, sugar, pepper and salt. Place the chops in the grill and cover each with the mustard orange sauce. Grill for 4–6 minutes, or according to your preference. Arrange the orange slices on 4 plates and place a lamb chop on top of each. Serves 4.

NUTRITIONAL ANALYSIS: Calories: 231 Total fat: 9 g Saturated fat: 3 g
% calories from fat: 36 Carbohydrates: 16 g Protein: 22 g Cholesterol: 67 mg Sodium: 568 mg

Garlic Lamb & New Potatoes

This recipe originated in Greece, where lamb is highly prized for it's tenderness and flavor.

4	4–6 oz. lamb loin chops	4	small new potatoes
2	cloves garlic, finely minced	4	fresh mushrooms, thinly sliced
2 T.	lemon juice	1 t.	olive oil
1 T.	olive oil	1 t.	salt
1 T.	fresh rosemary, finely minced	½ t.	black pepper
1 t.	black pepper, coarsely ground		nonfat cooking spray

Remove any visible fat from the chops and place the chops in a flat glass pan. Combine the garlic, lemon juice, oil, rosemary and 1 teaspoon of black pepper in a small bowl and pour over the chops. Cover tightly and marinate in the refrigerator for 2–8 hours. Scrub the potatoes and slice into ¼-inch rounds. Coat the grill with cooking spray and preheat for 5 minutes.

Place the potatoes and mushrooms in the grill and sprinkle with the olive oil, salt and pepper. Grill for 5 minutes. Move the potatoes and mushrooms to the sides of the grill and add the lamb chops. Grill the lamb and vegetables for 4–6 minutes, or until the chops are rare to medium and the potatoes are tender. Serves 4.

NUTRITIONAL ANALYSIS: Calories: 307 Total fat: 13 g Saturated fat: 4 g
% calories from fat: 37 Carbohydrates: 26 g Protein: 23 g Cholesterol: 67 mg Sodium: 636 mg

Raspberry & Mint Lamb Chops

A hint of sweetness complements the chops.

4	4–6 oz. lamb loin chops
2 T.	raspberry jelly
1 t.	fresh mint, finely minced
1 t.	olive oil
1	clove garlic, finely minced
	nonfat cooking spray

Remove any visible fat from the chops. Coat the grill with cooking spray and preheat for 5 minutes. In a small bowl, combine the jelly, mint, oil and garlic. Place the chops in the grill and spoon the sauce over each. Grill for 4–6 minutes. Serves 4.

NUTRITIONAL ANALYSIS: Calories: 191 Total fat: 9 g Saturated fat: 3 g
% calories from fat: 43 Carbohydrates: 7 g Protein: 20 g Cholesterol: 67 mg Sodium: 47 mg

Grilled Lamb Chops with Papaya Peach Salsa

Count on this tangy salsa to awaken your appetite!

4	4–6 oz. lamb loin chops
1 t.	black pepper, coarsely ground
½ t.	salt
2 c.	ripe papayas, chopped
1 c.	ripe peaches, chopped
1 T.	red onion, chopped
2 T.	fresh cilantro, chopped
1 T.	lemon juice
¼ t.	salt
	nonfat cooking spray

Remove all visible fat from the chops. Coat the grill with cooking spray and preheat for 5 minutes. Place the chops in the grill and sprinkle with the pepper and ½ teaspoon of salt. Grill for 4–6 minutes. In a medium serving bowl, mix together thoroughly the papayas, peaches, onion, cilantro, lemon juice and ½ teaspoon salt. To serve, place one lamp chop on each plate and cover with the salsa. Serves 4.

NUTRITIONAL ANALYSIS: Calories: 204 Total fat: 8 g Saturated fat: 3 g
% calories from fat: 35 Carbohydrates: 13 g Protein: 21 g Cholesterol: 67 mg Sodium: 481 mg

Moroccan Lamb Kebabs

These beautiful kebabs make any meal a special occasion.

1 lb.	boneless lamb	1	zucchini
1 T.	olive oil	12	mushrooms
2 T.	lemon juice	8	cherry tomatoes
2 T.	water	8	10-inch wooden skewers
2 T.	balsamic vinegar	1 t.	salt
1 t.	black pepper, coarsely ground	½ t.	black pepper
1	clove garlic, finely minced		nonfat cooking spray
1 t.	oregano		

Remove any visible fat from the lamb and cut into 1-inch cubes. In a small bowl, combine the oil, lemon juice, water, vinegar, pepper, garlic and oregano. Place the lamb in a flat glass pan and pour the marinade over the meat, turning the pieces to coat thoroughly. Refrigerate, covered, for 2–12 hours. Scrub the zucchini and cut into 1-inch cubes. Clean the mushrooms and tomatoes. Soak the wooden skewers in water for 20 minutes and pat dry. When ready to grill, thread the lamb and vegetables on the skewers, alternating each. Dust each skewer with salt and pepper. Coat the grill with cooking spray and preheat for 5 minutes. Grill the kebabs widthwise (horizontally) for 7–8 minutes, or according to your preference. Serves 4.

NUTRITIONAL ANALYSIS: Calories: 156 Total fat: 9 g Saturated fat: 2 g % calories from fat: 49 Carbohydrates: 9 g Protein: 12 g Cholesterol: 33 mg Sodium: 621 mg

CHAPTER 4

SMOKY SENSATIONS— PORK CHOPS, RIBS & HAM

If you've ever tried barbequed pork ribs, smoky and hot from the grill, you will understand why pork has grown in popularity over the past several years. Pork has an even texture and a mild taste that agrees with many ingredients. However, pork cuts differ wildly in fat content, ranging from 7 fat grams for a typical tenderloin to a whopping 56 fat grams for a standard serving of country-style pork ribs! In this chapter you'll find recipes that will highlight chops, ribs, tenderloin and ham, and we'll also offer some ways to reduce the fat in the pork as you prepare it.

Although food handling has improved in the past several years, you should still be prepared to grill pork until it is well done (about 160°) to avoid possible contamination. However, pork becomes dry and tough if you overcook it, so watch pork carefully as it grills. Check it a few minutes before it's supposed to be done and time it accordingly.

Ribs are a favorite pork specialty and we prepare them in our recipes by parboiling them first. To parboil ribs, they are steamed over boiling water for twenty minutes. This accomplishes two important purposes. First, it partially separates the meat from the fat on each rib, making it easier to remove the fat before grilling. And, parboiling "pre-cooks" the ribs by steaming, which helps to preserve the tenderness of the meat while it ensures that the pork is completely cooked before serving. Even though parboiling adds a bit of time to your preparation, we think you'll agree with us that the results are well worth it!

PORK TENDERLOIN & CHOPS

Grilled Pork with Peach Salsa
Marinated tenderloin combines with a snappy salsa!

4	6–8 oz. pork tenderloins		1 t.	ground ginger
1 t.	vegetable oil		¼ t.	ground cinnamon
1 T.	honey		2 T.	apricot marmalade
2 T.	low sodium soy sauce		3	peaches, peeled and cut into ½-inch pieces
1 T.	cider vinegar		¼ c.	chopped red onion
			2 T.	fresh parsley, minced
				nonfat cooking spray

Remove any visible fat from the pork. Place the pork in a flat glass pan. Combine the oil, honey, soy sauce and vinegar and pour over the pork. Cover tightly and refrigerate 1–8 hours. In a large serving bowl, combine the ginger, cinnamon, marmalade, peaches, onion and parsley. Toss lightly and refrigerate. Coat the grill with cooking spray and preheat for 5 minutes. Grill the tenderloins for 4–6 minutes, or according to your preference. To serve, spoon the salsa over the tenderloins. Serves 4.

NUTRITIONAL ANALYSIS: Calories: 278 Total fat: 7 g Saturated fat: 2 g
% calories from fat: 23 Carbohydrates: 20 g Protein: 37 g Cholesterol: 101 mg Sodium: 586 mg

Dijon Grilled Pork Tenderloin

This Dijon mustard sauce spices up the mild flavor of pork.

2	cloves garlic, finely minced
1 T.	Dijon mustard
1 t.	ground ginger
3 T.	lemon juice
1 T.	olive oil
1 t.	black pepper
½ t.	salt
4	6 oz. pork tenderloins
	nonfat cooking spray

Remove any visible fat from the pork. Lightly coat the grill with cooking spray and preheat for 5 minutes. In a small bowl, combine the garlic, mustard, ginger, lemon juice, oil, pepper and salt. Place the pork in the grill and generously brush with the Dijon mustard sauce. Grill for 4–6 minutes. Serves 4.

NUTRITIONAL ANALYSIS: Calories: 252 Total fat: 10 g Saturated fat: 3 g % calories from fat: 36 Carbohydrates: 3 g Protein: 36 g Cholesterol: 101 mg Sodium: 458 mg

Pineapple Marinated Pork

Sweet and juicy!

4	8 oz. pork tenderloins
2 c.	unsweetened pineapple juice
1 t.	ground cinnamon
1 t.	ground ginger
½ t.	salt
4	fresh pineapple slices, ½-inch thick (or 4 canned pineapple slices)
2 oz.	slivered almond pieces
2 T.	fresh cilantro, chopped
	nonfat cooking spray

Remove any visible fat from the pork and place the pork in a flat glass pan. Combine the pineapple juice, cinnamon, ginger and salt and pour over the pork. Cover tightly and refrigerate for 2–12 hours. Coat the grill with cooking spray and preheat for 5 minutes.

Grill the pork for 3 minutes. Top each tenderloin with 1 pineapple slice. Grill for 2–3 minutes, or according to your preference. Garnish each tenderloin with slivered almonds and cilantro and serve. Serves 4.

NUTRITIONAL ANALYSIS: Calories: 453 Total fat: 16 g Saturated fat: 4 g
% calories from fat: 32 Carbohydrates: 25 g Protein: 51 g Cholesterol: 134 mg Sodium: 388 mg

Sausage & Herb Stuffed Pork

A perfect Sunday dinner entrée.

½ lb.	lowfat sausage, uncooked, casings removed
½ c.	fresh breadcrumbs
2 T.	fresh parsley
½ t.	thyme
½ t.	marjoram
1 t.	black pepper, coarsely ground
4	6–8 oz. pork tenderloins
	nonfat cooking spray

Remove any visible fat from the pork. Coat the grill with cooking spray and preheat for 5 minutes. In a medium mixing bowl, combine the sausage, breadcrumbs, parsley, thyme, marjoram and pepper. With a sharp knife, cut a slit sideways almost completely through each tenderloin to create a pocket. Open the tenderloins and place one fourth of the sausage stuffing inside each. Press the edges of the pockets to close. Grill the tenderloins for 6–8 minutes, or until the pork and stuffing are completely cooked. With the plastic spatula, carefully scoop the pork from the grill. Serves 4.

NUTRITIONAL ANALYSIS: Calories: 366 Total fat: 11 g Saturated fat: 3 g % calories from fat: 29 Carbohydrates: 14 g Protein: 49 g Cholesterol: 141 mg Sodium: 446 mg

Quick & Easy Pork Tenderloins

A 15-minute entrée from start to finish!

4	6–8 oz. pork tenderloins
¼ c.	low sodium soy sauce
2 t.	ground ginger
4	green onions, chopped
1	clove garlic, chopped
½ t.	black pepper
	nonfat cooking spray

Remove all visible fat from the pork. Coat the grill with cooking spray and preheat for 5 minutes. Combine the soy sauce, ginger, green onions, garlic and pepper in a flat glass pan. Dip each tenderloin into the soy ginger sauce and place in the grill. Spoon 1 tablespoon of sauce over each tenderloin. Grill for 4–6 minutes, or according to your preference. Serves 4.

NUTRITIONAL ANALYSIS: Calories: 227 Total fat: 6 g Saturated fat: 2 g
% calories from fat: 26 Carbohydrates: 3 g Protein: 37 g Cholesterol: 101 mg Sodium: 607 mg

Caribbean Jerk Pork

A little spicy taste of the Caribbean!

1 lb.	pork tenderloin
1 T.	fresh ginger, grated
1 t.	black pepper, coarsely ground
1 T	brown sugar
2	cloves garlic, finely minced
2 T.	fresh cilantro, chopped
½ t.	cayenne pepper
¼ t.	nutmeg
¼ t.	coriander
	nonfat cooking spray

Remove all visible fat from the pork and place the tenderloin in a flat glass pan. In a small bowl, mix the ginger, pepper, brown sugar, garlic, cilantro, cayenne pepper, nutmeg and coriander. Blend well to make a thick rub. Press the rub firmly onto all sides of the pork and cover tightly. Refrigerate for 1–2 hours. Coat the grill with cooking spray and preheat for 5 minutes. Grill the pork for 4–6 minutes. To serve, slice thinly across the grain of the meat. Serves 4.

NUTRITIONAL ANALYSIS: Calories: 154　Total fat: 4 g　Saturated fat: 1 g　% calories from fat: 26　Carbohydrates: 4 g　Protein: 24 g　Cholesterol: 67 mg　Sodium: 49 mg

Grilled Pork with Barbeque Table Mop

These barbequed pork slices are served with a generous "mop," or dipping sauce, at the table. You may also serve these pork slices on toasted buns as a luncheon entrée.

1 lb.	pork tenderloin
1 t.	salt
½ t.	black pepper
8 oz.	low sodium tomato sauce
2 T.	prepared mustard
½ t.	Tabasco sauce
1 T.	brown sugar
1	clove garlic, finely minced
1	small onion, finely chopped
	nonfat cooking spray

Remove any visible fat from the pork and dust the tenderloin with the salt and pepper. In a small saucepan, combine the tomato sauce, mustard, Tabasco, brown sugar, garlic and onion and simmer for 20 minutes. Do not boil. Coat the grill with cooking spray and preheat for 5 minutes. Grill the tenderloin for 2 minutes. Generously "mop" the pork with the sauce. Continue grilling for 2–4 minutes. Watch the drip tray carefully, as the sauce will melt and run into the tray. To serve, slice thinly across the grain of the meat, heap pork slices on individual plates and cover with additional warm barbeque sauce. Serves 4.

NUTRITIONAL ANALYSIS: Calories: 198　Total fat: 5 g　Saturated fat: 1 g　% calories from fat: 23　Carbohydrates: 12 g　Protein: 26 g　Cholesterol: 67 mg　Sodium: 641 mg

Hungarian Paprika Pork Chops

Sweet paprika adds to the spicy rub for these chops.

4	6 oz. pork loin chops
1 t.	paprika
½ t.	salt
½ t.	black pepper
¼ t.	ground ginger
1 t.	garlic powder
¼ t.	dry mustard
	nonfat cooking spray

Remove all visible fat from the chops. Combine the paprika, salt, pepper, ginger, garlic powder and mustard and rub onto all sides of each chop. Coat the grill with cooking spray and preheat for 5 minutes. Grill the chops for 5–6 minutes. Serves 4.

NUTRITIONAL ANALYSIS: Calories: 234   Total fat: 8 g   Saturated fat: 3 g   % calories from fat: 32   Carbohydrates: 1 g   Protein: 37 g   Cholesterol: 108 mg   Sodium: 357 mg

Herbed Pork Chops & New Potatoes

This well-seasoned combination of pork and potatoes is marinated overnight.

4	4–6 oz. center cut pork chops
1 lb.	small red potatoes
1 c.	nonfat chicken broth
1 t.	dried rosemary, crumbled
½ t.	dried marjoram, crumbled
½ t.	dried sage, crumbled
1 t.	salt
1 t.	black pepper
1 T.	cider vinegar
	nonfat cooking spray

Remove any visible fat from the chops. Place the chops in a flat glass pan. Scrub the potatoes, cut into wedges and put in a resealable plastic bag. Mix together in a medium bowl the broth, rosemary, marjoram, sage, salt, pepper and vinegar. Pour one-half of the marinade over the chops and pour the remaining marinade into the plastic bag with the potatoes. Cover the chops tightly, seal the plastic bag and refrigerate both containers overnight. Coat the grill with cooking spray and preheat for 5 minutes. Place the potatoes in the grill and cook for 4 minutes. Push the potatoes to the sides of the grill and add the chops. Grill for 5–6 minutes. Serves 4.

NUTRITIONAL ANALYSIS: Calories: 216   Total fat: 5 g   Saturated fat: 2 g
% calories from fat: 21   Carbohydrates: 21 g   Protein: 21 g   Cholesterol: 50 mg   Sodium: 666 mg

Texas Barbeque Pork Chops

Always a favorite!

4	4–6 oz. center cut pork chops
½ t.	black pepper
½ c.	dark brown sugar
¾ c.	ketchup
1	onion, chopped
3	cloves garlic, finely chopped
1 t.	chili powder
	nonfat cooking spray

Remove all visible fat from the chops. In a small saucepan, combine the pepper, brown sugar, ketchup, onion, garlic and chili powder. Simmer for 15 minutes until slightly thickened. Lightly coat the grill with cooking spray and preheat for 5 minutes.

Place the chops in the grill and spoon 1 heaping tablespoon of sauce over each chop. Grill the chops for 5–6 minutes, watching carefully to avoid burning the sauce. Serve the cooked chops with the remaining warm sauce. Serves 4.

NUTRITIONAL ANALYSIS: Calories: 235 Total fat: 5 g Saturated fat: 2 g % calories from fat: 19 Carbohydrates: 30 g Protein: 19 g Cholesterol: 50 mg Sodium: 414 mg

Dijon Butter Pork Chops

The mustard butter adds a subtle, tangy flavor to the meat.

4	6 oz. shoulder pork chops
¼ c.	lowfat margarine
1 T.	Dijon mustard
1 t.	lemon juice
1 t.	fresh parsley, minced
1 T.	green onions, minced
¼ t.	paprika
½ t.	salt
½ t.	white pepper
	nonfat cooking spray

Remove any visible fat from the chops. In a small bowl, combine the margarine, mustard, lemon juice, parsley, green onions, paprika, salt and pepper. Blend well. Coat the grill with cooking spray and preheat for 5 minutes. Place the chops in the grill and top each with 1 tablespoon of the Dijon butter. The Dijon butter will melt and run into the drip tray as the chops grill. Grill for 5–6 minutes. To serve, assemble the chops on individual plates and pour the melted Dijon-butter over each chop. Serves 4.

NUTRITIONAL ANALYSIS: Calories: 357   Total fat: 18 g   Saturated fat: 5 g   % calories from fat: 45   Carbohydrates: 2 g   Protein: 46 g   Cholesterol: 138 mg   Sodium: 540 mg

Chili Rubbed Pork Chops

Extra spicy for robust flavor!

4	4–6 oz. pork loin chops
2 T.	chili powder
2 T.	brown sugar
½ t.	salt
½ t.	cumin
1 T.	black pepper, coarsely ground
	nonfat cooking spray

Remove all visible fat from the chops. Combine the chili powder, brown sugar, salt, cumin and pepper and generously rub onto all sides of each chop. Coat the grill with cooking spray and preheat for 5 minutes. Grill the chops for 5–6 minutes. Serves 4.

NUTRITIONAL ANALYSIS: Calories: 186   Total fat: 6 g   Saturated fat: 2 g   % calories from fat: 29   Carbohydrates: 8 g   Protein: 25 g   Cholesterol: 72 mg   Sodium: 375 mg

Teriyaki Pork & Rice Bowls

An appealing main dish for every member of the family.

3	6 oz. pork loin chops
2	green onions, finely chopped
½ c.	low sodium soy sauce
1 t.	ground ginger
2 T.	brown sugar
2 T.	rice vinegar
1	clove garlic, minced
2 c.	cooked long-grain white rice
	nonfat cooking spray

Remove any visible fat and the bone from the chops. Cut the pork into very thin slices and set aside. In a small saucepan, heat and blend the onions, soy sauce, ginger, brown sugar, vinegar and garlic to make the teriyaki sauce. Coat the grill with cooking spray and preheat for 5 minutes. Grill the pork slices for 3 minutes. Drizzle 2 tablespoons of sauce over the pork. Spoon the rice over the pork and pour the remaining sauce over the rice. The teriyaki sauce may melt and run into the drip tray. Grill for 2–3 minutes. Remove the pork and rice from the grill and serve in individual bowls, spooning any melted sauce over each. Serves 4.

NUTRITIONAL ANALYSIS: Calories: 276   Total fat: 6 g   Saturated fat: 2 g
% calories from fat: 20   Carbohydrates: 23 g   Protein: 31 g   Cholesterol: 81 mg   Sodium: 765 mg

PORK RIBS, SAUSAGE & HAM

New Orleans Pork Ribs

These boneless ribs take less time and effort to prepare than traditional ribs.

1½ lb.	boneless, country-style, pork ribs
¼ c.	tomato paste
¼ c.	cider vinegar
2 T.	honey
2 T.	water
1 T.	olive oil
2 t.	dry mustard
½ t.	Tabasco sauce
1	clove garlic, minced
¼ c.	onion, chopped
	nonfat cooking spray

Remove any visible fat from the ribs. Score the ribs with a knife to prevent the meat from curling as it grills. In a small saucepan, combine the remaining ingredients and blend until thickened, about 5 minutes, and keep warm. Coat the grill with cooking spray and pre-heat for 5 minutes. Place the ribs in the grill and cover each with 1 tablespoon of sauce. Grill for 6 minutes. Turn the ribs and baste each with 1 tablespoon of sauce. Grill for 2–4 minutes, or until cooked through. Serve with the remaining warm sauce. Serves 4.

NUTRITIONAL ANALYSIS: Calories: 401 Total fat: 21 g Saturated fat: 7 g
% calories from fat: 48 Carbohydrates: 17 g Protein: 36 g Cholesterol: 110 mg Sodium: 105 mg

Sweet n' Smoky Ribs

A tempting favorite Southern recipe.

4 lbs.	pork baby back ribs
2 T.	liquid hickory smoke
½ t.	black pepper
½ t.	salt
1	clove garlic, minced
2 T.	olive oil
¼ c.	ketchup
1 T.	cider vinegar
1 T.	sugar
¼ c.	orange juice
	nonfat cooking spray

Slice the ribs into individual pieces. Parboil the ribs for 20 minutes. (To parboil ribs: cook the ribs for 20 minutes in a steamer rack over a pan of boiling water). Cool and remove any visible fat. Place the ribs in a flat glass pan. Combine the liquid smoke, pepper, salt, garlic, oil, ketchup, vinegar, sugar and orange juice and pour over the ribs. Cover tightly and refrigerate for 2–8 hours. Coat the grill with cooking spray and preheat for 5 minutes. Discard the marinade and place the ribs in the grill in a single layer. Grill for 5–7 minutes. Keep the cooked ribs warm on a serving platter while grilling any remaining ribs. Serves 6.

NUTRITIONAL ANALYSIS: Calories: 600 Total fat: 35 g Saturated fat: 12 g % calories from fat: 54 Carbohydrates: 7 g Protein: 59 g Cholesterol: 195 mg Sodium: 458 mg

Grilled Italian Sausage & Peppers

Choose from a variety of lowfat sausages to make this dish memorable.

2 lbs.	lowfat Italian pork sausage (or any other lowfat sausage)
2	green peppers, seeded and thinly sliced
1	onion, thinly sliced
1 t.	black pepper
½ t.	salt
	nonfat cooking spray

Cut the sausage into 4 portions. Lightly spray the grill with cooking spray and preheat for 5 minutes. Place the sausage, peppers and onion in the grill and dust with pepper and salt. Grill for 5–6 minutes. Serves 4.

NUTRITIONAL ANALYSIS: Calories: 430 Total fat: 18 g Saturated fat: 5 g
% calories from fat: 36 Carbohydrates: 23 g Protein: 48 g Cholesterol: 161 mg Sodium: 936 mg

Sausage & Vegetable Mixed Grill

Perfect for a cold winter evening.

4	baking potatoes
1	onion
1 t.	oregano
½ t.	Italian seasoning
½ t.	black pepper
2 lbs.	lowfat pork sausage links
	nonfat cooking spray

Coat the grill with cooking spray and preheat for 5 minutes. Scrub the potatoes and cut into thin wedges. Peel and thinly slice the onion. Place the potatoes and onion in the grill and dust with the oregano, Italian seasoning and pepper. Grill for 3 minutes. Add the sausages and grill for 5–6 minutes, or until the sausages are cooked and the vegetables are tender. Serves 4.

NUTRITIONAL ANALYSIS: Calories: 549 Total fat: 18 g Saturated fat: 5 g
% calories from fat: 29 Carbohydrates: 50 g Protein: 50 g Cholesterol: 161 mg Sodium: 660 mg

Applesauce Honey Ham

A quick and pleasing family entrée.

2 lbs.	lowfat ham steaks, cut into 8 portions
½ c.	applesauce, unsweetened
2 T.	clover honey
1 t.	ground ginger
½ t.	cinnamon
	nonfat cooking spray

Remove any visible fat from the steaks. Coat the grill with cooking spray and preheat for 5 minutes. In a small bowl, combine the applesauce, honey, ginger and cinnamon. Place the ham in the grill and top with the applesauce honey mixture. The applesauce honey mixture will melt and run into the drip tray. Grill the ham for 3–4 minutes, or until heated through. Watch carefully to make sure the applesauce does not burn. To serve, place the ham on individual plates and top with the melted applesauce. Serves 8.

NUTRITIONAL ANALYSIS: Calories: 142 Total fat: 4 g Saturated fat: 1 g
% calories from fat: 27 Carbohydrates: 9 g Protein: 17 g Cholesterol: 40 mg Sodium: 1,216 mg

TENDER CHOICES FROM THE SEA —FISH & SHELLFISH

Fish and shellfish offer a wide variety of flavors and textures—a bounty of delicious tastes, just waiting to be explored! Whether you choose a delicate and tender fillet of sole with a fresh lemon sauce, a thick grilled salmon steak, or spicy jumbo shrimp skewers, fish and shellfish are a delicious way to pack protein and essential nutrients into your diet.

Marinades and sauces work well with fish prepared in the grill. Depending on the type of fish, you can select fruit, tomato, or herb sauces to accompany it. Many types of fish have a firm texture, such as salmon and swordfish, which partner especially well with sauces. One of our favorite recipes in this chapter is Thai Salmon Steak, which grills with a crisp, sweet honey-mustard glaze. A perfect combination of tender fish and a tangy accompaniment!

If you've never spent much time preparing fish before, take a quick look at the recipes that follow. You'll find that the *George Foreman Grilling Machine* will make it easy for you, as it grills on both sides and evenly distributes the heat. You may want to prepare the non-stick surface of the grill by spraying it with a nonfat cooking spray and watch the drip tray, as the melted sauces and marinades will collect in the tray. Choose from any of the recipes that follow and stand back to receive the compliments!

FISH FILLETS & STEAKS

Pacific Northwest Salmon Steaks

This exquisite honey-dill sauce creates an unforgettable entrée!

¼ c.	clover honey
2 t.	fresh dill, finely minced
2 t.	fresh parsley, finely minced
1 T.	lowfat butter
¼ t.	salt
4	6 oz. salmon steaks
	nonfat cooking spray

Coat the grill with cooking spray and preheat for 5 minutes. In a small saucepan, heat the honey, dill, parsley, butter and salt until simmering. Grill the salmon steaks for 4 minutes. Spoon the honey-dill sauce over each steak and continue grilling for 2–4 minutes. As the sauce melts, it may run into the drip tray. To serve, drizzle any melted sauce from the tray over the steaks. Serves 4.

NUTRITIONAL ANALYSIS: Calories: 442 Total fat: 22 g Saturated fat: 5 g
% calories from fat: 46 Carbohydrates: 18 g Protein: 41 g Cholesterol: 107 mg Sodium: 288 mg

Spicy Citrus Tuna

The marinade adds flavor and tenderizes the tuna.

4	6 oz. tuna steaks
½ c.	unsweetened pineapple juice
½ c.	unsweetened orange juice
½ c.	unsweetened grapefruit juice
½ t.	salt
½ t.	black pepper
2 t.	paprika
¼ t.	cayenne pepper
	nonfat cooking spray

Place the tuna in a flat glass pan. Combine the pineapple juice, orange juice, grapefruit juice, salt, black pepper, paprika and cayenne pepper in a small bowl and pour over the steaks. Cover the fish tightly and refrigerate for 1–2 hours. Lightly coat the grill with the cooking spray and preheat for 5 minutes. Grill the steaks for 6–8 minutes, or according to your preference. Discard any unused marinade. Serves 4.

NUTRITIONAL ANALYSIS: Calories: 311 Total fat: 5 g Saturated fat: >1 g
% calories from fat: 15 Carbohydrates: 12 g Protein: 52 g Cholesterol: 99 mg Sodium: 372 mg

Florentine Tuna

A fresh tomato and spinach pasta accompanies the tuna.

1	bunch fresh spinach
1	ripe tomato, chopped
2 T.	olive oil
1	clove garlic, finely minced
1 T.	fresh parsley, finely minced
1 T.	cider vinegar
1 t.	salt
½ t.	black pepper, coarsely ground
4	6–8 oz. tuna steaks
8 oz.	vermicelli noodles, cooked and drained
	nonfat cooking spray

Rinse the spinach greens and steam for 5 minutes on the stove over medium heat. Cool and chop finely. Coat the grill with the cooking spray and pre-heat for 5 minutes. In a medium saucepan, combine the chopped spinach, tomato, oil, garlic, parsley, vinegar, salt and pepper. Simmer for 10 minutes. Grill the tuna steaks for 6–8 minutes, or until the fish flakes easily. Divide the vermicelli among four individual plates, spoon the sauce over each and top with the grilled tuna. Serves 4.

NUTRITIONAL ANALYSIS: Calories: 432   Total fat: 12 g   Saturated fat: 2 g
% calories from fat: 26   Carbohydrates: 22 g   Protein: 57 g   Cholesterol: 99 mg   Sodium: 732 mg

Cajun Rubbed Red Snapper

Snapper has a mild, subtle flavor that makes it a perfect partner for this lively Cajun rub.

½ t.	paprika
½ t.	cayenne pepper
¼ t.	salt
¼ t.	black pepper
¼ t.	garlic powder
¼ t.	onion powder
1 T.	fresh parsley, finely minced
4	6 oz. red snapper fillets
	nonfat cooking spray

Lightly coat the grill with cooking spray and preheat for 5 minutes. In a small plastic bag, mix the paprika, cayenne pepper, salt, black pepper, garlic powder, onion powder and parsley. Shake well and pour onto a plate. Press the fillets into the rub and turn to cover thoroughly. Grill the snapper for 3–5 minutes, or until the fish flakes easily. Serves 4.

NUTRITIONAL ANALYSIS: Calories: 248 Total fat: 6 g Saturated fat: >1 g
% calories from fat: 22 Carbohydrates: 1 g Protein: 45 g Cholesterol: 80 mg Sodium: 243 mg

Santa Fe Sea Bass

Fresh garden vegetables bring out the best of sea bass.

½	green pepper, seeded, diced	1 T.	lime juice
½	red pepper, seeded, diced	1 T.	lemon juice
½	yellow pepper, seeded, diced	1 t.	olive oil
½	small onion, diced	1 t.	black pepper, coarsely ground
½ c.	corn (fresh cooked or canned)	½ t.	salt
		4	6 oz. sea bass fillets
			nonfat cooking spray

In a medium bowl, combine the peppers, onion, corn, lime juice, lemon juice, oil, pepper and salt, mixing the vegetables with the seasonings. Lightly coat the grill with the cooking spray and preheat for 5 minutes. Place the vegetables in the grill and cook for 3 minutes. Add the sea bass fillets to the vegetable mixture, placing the vegetables around the fish in the grill. Grill for 3–5 minutes, or until fish flakes easily and the vegetables are tender-crisp. Serves 4.

NUTRITIONAL ANALYSIS: Calories: 282 Total fat: 9 g Saturated fat: 2 g
% calories from fat: 28 Carbohydrates: 9 g Protein: 41 g Cholesterol: 90 mg Sodium: 152 mg

Thai Salmon Steaks

Wonderfully sweet and tangy flavors!

1 t.	rice vinegar
2 T.	low sodium soy sauce
¼ c.	honey
2 T.	Chinese mustard
2 T.	fresh parsley, finely minced
4	6 oz. salmon steaks
	nonfat cooking spray

In a small saucepan, combine the vinegar, soy sauce, honey, mustard and parsley. Simmer for 5 minutes. Coat the grill with the cooking spray and preheat for 5 minutes. Place the steaks in the grill and cover each with a spoonful of the Thai sauce. Grill for 6–8 minutes, or until the salmon flakes easily. Serve with any remaining sauce. Serves 4.

NUTRITIONAL ANALYSIS: Calories: 401 Total fat: 17 g Saturated fat: 4 g
% calories from fat: 39 Carbohydrates: 19 g Protein: 42 g Cholesterol: 107 mg Sodium: 454 mg

Lemon Basil Halibut

A healthful and elegant entrée for guests.

4	6 oz. halibut steaks
1 t.	paprika
½ c.	lowfat margarine
1 T.	fresh basil, finely minced
1 T.	lemon juice
1 T.	green onion, finely minced
	nonfat cooking spray

Lightly coat the grill with cooking spray and preheat for 5 minutes. Place the steaks in the grill and sprinkle with the paprika. Grill for 6–8 minutes, or until fish flakes easily. In a small bowl, blend the margarine, basil, lemon juice and green onion. To serve, arrange each steak on a plate and top with a generous spoonful of the lemon-basil butter. Serves 4.

NUTRITIONAL ANALYSIS: Calories: 325 Total fat: 11 g Saturated fat: 2 g
% calories from fat: 33 Carbohydrates: 4 g Protein: 46 g Cholesterol: 70 mg Sodium: 271 mg

Grilled Swordfish with Fresh Tomato Herb Couli

A smooth sauce of tomato and herbs accents the swordfish.

1 t.	olive oil		½ t.	ground oregano
1 T.	lemon juice		½ t.	dried thyme
3	ripe tomatoes, chopped		¼ t.	dried rosemary
¼ c.	tomato sauce		½ t.	black pepper
3 T.	onion, chopped		½ t.	salt
½ c.	fresh bread crumbs		4	8 oz. swordfish steaks
½ t.	black pepper		2 T.	fresh parsley, finely chopped
				nonfat cooking spray

Place the oil, lemon juice, tomatoes, tomato sauce, onion, bread crumbs, oregano, thyme, rosemary, pepper and salt in a blender and pulse until very smooth and thick. Refrigerate until ready to use. Lightly coat the grill with cooking spray and preheat for 5 minutes. Grill the swordfish for 6–9 minutes, or until the fish flakes easily. To serve, pour one-fourth of the sauce onto each of 4 dinner plates, top with the steaks and garnish with the parsley. Serves 4.

NUTRITIONAL ANALYSIS: Calories: 295 Total fat: 11 g Saturated fat: 2 g % calories from fat: 34 Carbohydrates: 15 g Protein: 34 g Cholesterol: 60 mg Sodium: 633 mg

Quick & Easy Halibut Fillets

The perfect answer to a busy day.

1 t.	olive oil
2 T.	lemon juice
1	clove garlic, finely minced
1 T.	fresh parsley, finely minced
1 t.	black pepper, coarsely ground
4	6 oz. halibut fillets
	nonfat cooking spray

Coat the grill with cooking spray and preheat for 5 minutes. In a small bowl, combine the oil, lemon juice, garlic, parsley and black pepper. Place the fillets in the grill, drizzle the lemon sauce over each and grill for 4–6 minutes, or until the fish flakes easily. Serves 4.

NUTRITIONAL ANALYSIS: Calories: 280 Total fat: 9g Saturated fat: 1g % calories from fat: 30 Carbohydrates: 2 g Protein: 46 g Cholesterol: 70 mg Sodium: 118 mg

Orange Pressed Tuna

The sweet juice of the orange grills into the tuna!

4	6 oz. tuna steaks
1	fresh orange
1 t.	fresh parsley, finely minced
½ t.	salt
¼ t.	black pepper
	nonfat cooking spray

Lightly coat the grill with cooking spray and preheat for 5 minutes. Peel and slice the orange into ¼-inch thick slices. Place the tuna in the grill and sprinkle the parsley, salt and pepper over each steak. Cover with the orange slices. Grill for 6–8 minutes, or until the fish flakes easily. Discard the grilled orange slices and serve. Serves 4.

NUTRITIONAL ANALYSIS: Calories: 279 Total fat: 5 g Saturated fat: >1 g % calories from fat: 17 Carbohydrates: 4 g Protein: 51 g Cholesterol: 99 mg Sodium: 371 mg

Orange Roughy Primavera

Orange roughy is sweet, mild and very delicate.

1	zucchini
1	red pepper
1	onion
1	carrot
1 t.	fresh rosemary, minced
1 t.	fresh thyme, minced
1 t.	black pepper, coarsely ground
1 t.	olive oil
4	6 oz. orange roughy fillets
	nonfat cooking spray

Coat the grill with cooking spray and preheat for 5 minutes. Thinly slice the zucchini, red pepper, onion and carrot. In a small bowl, combine the rosemary, thyme, pepper and oil. Place the vegetables in the grill and drizzle one half of the herb oil over them. Grill for 5 minutes. Move the vegetables to the sides of the grill and add the fillets. Drizzle the remaining herb oil over the fillets. Grill for 4–6 minutes, or until the fish flakes easily and the vegetables are tender. To serve, carefully remove the fillets from the grill and top with the vegetables. Serves 4.

NUTRITIONAL ANALYSIS: Calories: 223 Total fat: 6 g Saturated fat: >1 g % calories from fat: 23 Carbohydrates: 8 g Protein: 34 g Cholesterol: 44 mg Sodium: 150 mg

Halibut with Avocado Lemon Cream

The creamy flavor of avocados makes this halibut memorable!

1	Haas avocado
1 T.	lemon juice
½ c.	nonfat cream cheese
4	6 oz. halibut steaks
1 t.	black pepper, coarsely ground
1 t.	salt
1 T.	lemon juice
	nonfat cooking spray

In a small bowl, peel and mash the avocado until smooth. Stir in the lemon juice and cream cheese and blend thoroughly. Refrigerate. Coat the grill with the cooking spray and preheat for 5 minutes. Place the halibut in the grill and sprinkle with the pepper, salt and lemon juice. Grill for 6–8 minutes, or until the fish flakes easily. To serve, top each fillet with one-fourth of the avocado cream. Serves 4.

NUTRITIONAL ANALYSIS: Calories: 374 Total fat: 15 g Saturated fat: 2 g
% calories from fat: 38 Carbohydrates: 9 g Protein: 49 g Cholesterol: 70 mg Sodium: 734 mg

Grilled Oriental Tuna

Serve rare to medium rare for best results.

2 T.	low sodium soy sauce
¼ c.	Asian hoisin sauce
1 t.	honey
1 t.	sesame oil
1 t.	Szechwan chile sauce
4	6 oz. tuna steaks
	nonfat cooking spray

In a small bowl, combine the soy sauce, hoisin sauce, honey, sesame oil and chile sauce. Place the tuna in a flat glass pan and spoon the sauce over each steak. Refrigerate, covered, for 1 hour. Lightly coat the grill with cooking spray and preheat for 5 minutes. Grill the steaks for 6–8 minutes, or according to your preference. Serves 4.

NUTRITIONAL ANALYSIS: Calories: 320 Total fat: 7 g Saturated fat: 1 g % calories from fat: 19 Carbohydrates: 10 g Protein: 52 g Cholesterol: 99 mg Sodium: 872 mg

Italian Rubbed Sea Bass Fillets

From the shores of Southern Italy.

2 t.	chili powder
1 T.	paprika
1	clove garlic, finely minced
¼ c.	fresh cilantro, finely minced
½ t.	black pepper, coarsely ground
1 t.	salt
4	6 oz. sea bass fillets
	nonfat cooking spray

In a small plastic bag, mix together the chili powder, paprika, garlic, cilantro, pepper and salt. Shake well and pour onto a plate. Place each fillet on the plate and press lightly to absorb the spices. Coat the grill with cooking spray and preheat for 5 minutes. Grill the fillets for 3–5 minutes. Serves 4.

NUTRITIONAL ANALYSIS: Calories: 249   Total fat: 8 g   Saturated fat: 1 g   % calories from fat: 28   Carbohydrates: 3 g   Protein: 41 g   Cholesterol: 90 mg   Sodium: 744 mg

Mango Orange Mahi-Mahi

For a very special occasion.

3 c.	mangos, chopped
2	green onions, finely chopped
1 T.	fresh parsley, finely minced
3 T.	orange juice
4	6–7 oz. mahi-mahi fillets
	nonfat cooking spray

In a medium bowl, combine the mangos, onions, parsley and orange juice. Refrigerate. Lightly coat the grill with cooking spray and preheat for 5 minutes. Grill the mahi-mahi for 3–5 minutes, or until fish flakes easily. Divide the mango salsa into 4 equal portions and serve on top of the fish. Serves 4.

NUTRITIONAL ANALYSIS: Calories: 261 Total fat: 4 g Saturated fat: >1 g
% calories from fat: 15 Carbohydrates: 24 g Protein: 32 g Cholesterol: 124 mg Sodium: 153 mg

SHELLFISH

Cilantro Lime-Dipped Shrimp

Grilled to perfection with just a hint of Mexican spices.

2 t.	olive oil
¼ c.	lime juice
2 T.	fresh cilantro, finely chopped
¼ t.	cayenne pepper
½ t.	salt
½ t.	black pepper
16	jumbo uncooked shrimp, peeled, deveined, tails removed
4	8-inch wooden skewers, soaked in water and drained
	nonfat cooking spray

Mix the oil, lime juice, cilantro, cayenne pepper, salt and pepper to make a marinade. Place the shrimp in the marinade and refrigerate for 1–2 hours. Coat the grill with cooking spray and preheat for 5 minutes. Arrange 4 shrimp on each skewer and grill widthwise (horizontally) for 1½–2½ minutes. Serves 4.

NUTRITIONAL ANALYSIS: Calories: 77 Total fat: 5 g Saturated fat: >1 g
% calories from fat: 62 Carbohydrates: 2 g Protein: 5 g Cholesterol: 47 mg Sodium: 345 mg

Surf & Sea Kebabs

These kebabs are delicious and amazingly lowfat!

12	large uncooked shrimp, peeled, deveined, tails removed
½ lb.	halibut, cut into 1-inch cubes
1	red pepper, cut into 1-inch pieces
½	purple onion, cut into 1-inch pieces
2 T.	lowfat margarine
1 t.	black pepper, coarsely ground
1 t.	seasoned salt
8	10-inch wooden skewers, soaked in water and drained
	nonfat cooking spray

Thread the shrimp and halibut with the red pepper and onion onto the skewers, alternating each. In a small bowl, combine the margarine, pepper and seasoned salt. Lightly coat the grill with the cooking spray and preheat for 5 minutes. Place the kebabs in the grill widthwise (horizontally) and brush with the seasoned butter. Grill the fish and vegetables for 4–7 minutes, or until the fish flakes easily and the vegetables are tender. As the butter melts, it will run into the drip tray. If desired, you may serve any melted sauce as an accompaniment to the grilled kebabs. Serves 4.

NUTRITIONAL ANALYSIS: Calories: 152 Total fat: 6 g Saturated fat: >1 g
% calories from fat: 34 Carbohydrates: 4 g Protein: 19 g Cholesterol: 58 mg Sodium: 466 mg

Vietnamese Lettuce-Wrapped Shrimp

This simple dish uses shrimp sparingly, but doesn't skimp on flavor!

16	large uncooked shrimp, peeled, deveined, tails removed
½ t.	Asian chile oil
¼ t.	black pepper
1 T.	sesame oil
1 T.	low sodium soy sauce
24	leaves of butter lettuce, rinsed
2 c.	carrots, grated
2 c.	bean sprouts, rinsed and cut into 1-inch pieces
¼ c.	hoisin sauce
4	8-inch wooden skewers, soaked in water and drained
	nonfat cooking spray

Thread the shrimp onto the skewers. Lightly coat the grill with cooking spray and preheat for 5 minutes. Combine the chile oil, pepper, sesame oil and soy sauce. Place the skewers in the grill widthwise (horizontally) and brush with the oil and pepper sauce. Grill the shrimp for 1½–2½ minutes. To serve, place equal portions of lettuce, carrots and bean sprouts on individual plates. Remove the shrimp from the skewers and add to each plate. Place a tablespoon of hoisin sauce on each plate. To assemble, place shrimp, carrots and bean sprouts on a lettuce leaf and roll up, tucking in the ends. Dip the lettuce wraps in the hoisin sauce as desired. Serves 4.

NUTRITIONAL ANALYSIS: Calories: 169 Total fat: 8 g Saturated fat: 1 g
% calories from fat: 40 Carbohydrates: 18 g Protein: 9 g Cholesterol: 47 mg Sodium: 594 mg

Scallops en Brochette

Serve with steamed spinach and angel hair pasta for an easy meal.

24	sea scallops
2 t.	olive oil
2 T.	white vinegar
¼ c.	low sodium soy sauce
1 t.	ground ginger
1	clove garlic, finely minced
1 T.	fresh parsley, finely minced
4	10-inch wooden skewers, soaked in water and drained
	nonfat cooking spray

Clean the scallops and place in a resealable plastic bag. Combine the oil, vinegar, soy sauce, ginger, garlic and parsley together and pour over the scallops. Seal the bag and refrigerate 2–6 hours. Lightly coat the grill with cooking spray and preheat for 5 minutes. Thread the scallops on the skewers and grill widthwise (horizontally) for 4–6 minutes, or until the scallops are opaque. Watch carefully to avoid overcooking. Discard any remaining marinade. Serves 4.

NUTRITIONAL ANALYSIS: Calories: 95 Total fat: 4 g Saturated fat: >1 g
% calories from fat: 40 Carbohydrates: 3 g Protein: 11 g Cholesterol: 19 mg Sodium: 781 mg

CHAPTER 6

SAVORY GRILLED POULTRY— CHICKEN & TURKEY

Whether you plan a weeknight family dinner or a special holiday meal, chances are chicken or turkey will almost always be found on your menu. Why? Poultry is full of flavor, easy to prepare and enjoyable to eat. Families consistently give chicken a "two-thumbs-up" review when it is grilled and served with herbs, spices, sauces or salsas. Almost any poultry choice is a winner!

Grilling brings out the best of poultry and the recipes that follow have their origins in countries all over the world. You'll find Mexican, Caribbean, Italian, French and Japanese spices and herbs used in these recipes. In addition, we've included some "down home" recipes such as Old Retreat Glazed Chicken Breasts and Sage-Stuffed Chicken Breasts that are reminiscent of classic dishes from the past.

You probably already know that chicken and turkey breast meat are among the lowest fat and highest protein choices, but you may not know that the skin of both has a high fat content and should be discarded. The recipes here call for skinless, boneless chicken and turkey meat. You may use frozen or fresh poultry, but be sure to thaw frozen poultry in the refrigerator and safely handle all raw poultry to avoid contamination. Poultry should be completely cooked to 170–180° and juices should run clear. Use nonfat cooking spray to coat the grill before adding the poultry and watch carefully to make sure you do not overcook the meat.

Fajita Rubbed Chicken

This grilled chicken makes a delicious start for tacos or fajitas.

1 T.	chili powder
½ t.	cayenne pepper
1 T.	fresh parsley, minced
1 T.	brown sugar
½ t.	black pepper
¼ t.	cumin
4	boneless, skinless chicken breast halves
	nonfat cooking spray

Combine the chili powder, cayenne pepper, parsley, brown sugar, pepper and cumin on a large plate. Mix the spices thoroughly. Press each chicken breast into the spices on all sides. Coat the grill with cooking spray and preheat for 5 minutes. Grill the chicken for 5–7 minutes. Serves 4.

NUTRITIONAL ANALYSIS: Calories: 348 Total fat: 10 g Saturated fat: 2 g
% calories from fat: 26 Carbohydrates: 7 g Protein: 56 g Cholesterol: 146 mg Sodium: 197 mg

Dijon Grilled Chicken Breasts

Tangy mustard is the perfect partner for chicken.

1 T.	Dijon mustard
1 T.	nonfat mayonnaise
1 t.	cider vinegar
1 t.	black pepper
½ t.	salt
1	clove garlic, minced
4	boneless, skinless chicken breast halves
	nonfat cooking spray

In a small bowl, mix together the mustard, mayonnaise, vinegar, pepper, salt and garlic. Lightly coat the grill with the cooking spray and preheat for 5 minutes. Place the chicken in the grill, spoon the sauce over each breast and grill for 5–7 minutes. Serves 4.

NUTRITIONAL ANALYSIS: Calories: 325 Total fat: 9 g Saturated fat: 2 g
% calories from fat: 26 Carbohydrates: 2 g Protein: 56 g Cholesterol: 146 mg Sodium: 535 mg

Japanese Soy Chicken

*Serve with Japanese stir-fry vegetables and steamed brown rice
for a delicious and healthy meal.*

¼ c.	low sodium soy sauce
1 t.	vegetable oil
1 t.	Asian chile oil
1	clove garlic, minced
1 t.	ground ginger
½ t.	black pepper
1 t.	clover honey
4	boneless, skinless chicken breast halves
	nonfat cooking spray

In a flat glass pan, combine the soy sauce, oils, garlic, ginger, pepper and honey. Mix well to dissolve the honey. Add the chicken breasts and turn to coat. Cover and refrigerate 1–4 hours. Coat the grill with cooking spray and preheat for 5 minutes. Grill the chicken for 5–7 minutes. Serves 4.

NUTRITIONAL ANALYSIS: Calories: 181 Total fat: 5 g Saturated fat: 1 g
% calories from fat: 27 Carbohydrates: 4 g Protein: 28 g Cholesterol: 73 mg Sodium: 593 mg

Sweet & Spicy Barbeque Chicken

Divide this sauce—use half for grilling and half as a table sauce.

1	15 oz. can tomato sauce
2	cloves garlic, finely minced
1 t.	olive oil
1	onion, finely chopped
2 T.	Worcestershire sauce
1 t.	chili powder
2 T.	cider vinegar
4	boneless, skinless chicken breast halves
	nonfat cooking spray

Combine the tomato sauce, garlic, oil, onion, Worcestershire sauce, chili powder and vinegar in a small saucepan. Heat and stir for 5 minutes. Remove ½ cup of the sauce and keep the remainder at a warm temperature, but do not boil. Lightly coat the grill with the cooking spray and preheat for 5 minutes. Add the chicken and spoon the ½ cup of sauce evenly over the breasts. Grill for 5–7 minutes. Pass the warmed sauce with the grilled chicken. Serves 4.

NUTRITIONAL ANALYSIS: Calories: 238 Total fat: 7g Saturated fat: 1g % calories from fat: 27 Carbohydrates: 14 g Protein: 30 g Cholesterol: 73 mg Sodium: 794 mg

Tamari Lemon Chicken

This entrée is easy to prepare and impressive when served.
You'll find tamari, an aged soy sauce, in the Oriental section of the grocery store.

1 T.	tamari
1 T.	fresh parsley, finely minced
2 T.	olive oil
3 T.	lemon juice
1 T.	black pepper, coarsely ground
6	boneless, skinless chicken breast halves
	nonfat cooking spray

In a small bowl, combine the tamari, parsley, oil, lemon juice and pepper. Coat the grill with cooking spray and preheat for 5 minutes. Place the chicken in the grill and drizzle each piece with the tamari lemon sauce. Grill the chicken for 5–7 minutes. Serves 6.

NUTRITIONAL ANALYSIS: Calories: 207 Total fat: 7 g Saturated fat: 1 g
% calories from fat: 18 Carbohydrates: 2 g Protein: 28 g Cholesterol: 73 mg Sodium: 172 mg

Jerk Chicken with Cilantro Rice

Perfect for a weekend supper.

½ c.	lemon juice		2 c.	long grain rice, cooked
2 T.	Szechwan chili sauce		2 T.	fresh cilantro, finely chopped
1 T.	fresh parsley, minced		2 T.	green onion, sliced
2 T.	vegetable oil		1	carrot, shredded
1 t.	paprika			nonfat cooking spray
1 T.	prepared mustard			
4	boneless, skinless chicken breast halves			

Lightly coat the grill with the cooking spray and preheat for 5 minutes. Combine the lemon juice, chili sauce, parsley, oil, paprika and mustard in a small bowl. Place the chicken breasts in the grill and spoon the jerk sauce over each piece. Grill for 5–7 minutes. Watch the drip tray carefully, as the sauce will melt and run into the tray.

Remove the chicken from the grill and keep warm. In a large bowl, combine the rice, cilantro, green onion and carrot. Coat the grill with cooking spray again and turn the rice onto the grill. Drizzle the melted sauce over the rice and grill for 3–4 minutes. To serve, arrange the rice on a large platter and top with the chicken breasts. Serves 4.

NUTRITIONAL ANALYSIS: Calories: 361 Total fat: 10 g Saturated fat: 2 g
% calories from fat: 25 Carbohydrates: 38 g Protein: 32 g Cholesterol: 73 mg Sodium: 194 mg

Hoisin-Glazed Chicken Thighs

Sweet and tangy hoisin sauce is readily available in the Oriental section of the grocery store.

8	boneless, skinless chicken thighs
¼ c.	hoisin sauce
2 T.	prepared barbeque sauce
1 T.	Worcestershire sauce
1	green onion, chopped
	nonfat cooking spray

Remove any visible fat from the chicken. Place the thighs in a flat glass pan. Combine the hoisin sauce, barbeque sauce, Worcestershire sauce and green onion and pour over the thighs. Cover tightly and refrigerate for 1–12 hours. Coat the grill with cooking spray and preheat for 5 minutes. Discard the marinade and grill the thighs for 5–7 minutes. Serves 4–6.

NUTRITIONAL ANALYSIS: Calories: 143 Total fat: 4 g Saturated fat: >1 g
% calories from fat: 27 Carbohydrates: 7 g Protein: 18 g Cholesterol: 76 mg Sodium: 348 mg

Indian Coriander Chicken

This chicken is sweet, tender and juicy!

4	boneless, skinless chicken breast halves
½ c.	lemon juice
¼ c.	water
1 t.	black pepper
1 t.	ground coriander
½ t.	ground cloves
½ t.	ground bay leaves
1 t.	salt
	nonfat cooking spray

Place the chicken in a flat glass pan. In a small bowl, combine the lemon juice, water, pepper, coriander, cloves, bay leaves and salt. Pour the marinade over the chicken, cover tightly and refrigerate for 1–12 hours. Coat the grill with cooking spray and preheat for 5 minutes. Place the breasts in the grill and cook for 5–7 minutes. Serves 4.

NUTRITIONAL ANALYSIS: Calories: 183   Total fat: 4 g   Saturated fat: 1 g
% calories from fat: 29   Carbohydrates: 4 g   Protein: 28 g   Cholesterol: 73 mg   Sodium: 643 mg

Old Retreat Glazed Chicken Breasts

This barbeque glaze holds just a hint of maple syrup for sweetness.

1	small onion, finely chopped
1	15 oz. can tomato sauce
1 T.	prepared mustard
2 T.	cider vinegar
¼ c.	maple syrup
1 t.	Worcestershire sauce
6	boneless, skinless chicken breast halves
	nonfat cooking spray

In a medium saucepan, combine the onion, tomato sauce, mustard, vinegar, maple syrup and Worcestershire sauce. Heat and simmer for 15 minutes. Coat the grill with cooking spray and preheat for 5 minutes. Place the breasts in the grill and spoon 1 tablespoon of the sauce over each piece. Grill for 2 minutes. Open the grill and spoon the sauce over the chicken again. Grill for 4–5 minutes. Pass the remaining sauce with the chicken. Serves 6.

NUTRITIONAL ANALYSIS: Calories: 225 Total fat: 5 g Saturated fat: 1 g
% calories from fat: 20 Carbohydrates: 16 g Protein: 29 g Cholesterol: 73 mg Sodium: 531 mg

Turkey Aglia Olio

A simple Italian farmer's dinner made especially good by adding tender grilled turkey.

1 lb.	boneless, skinless turkey breast
2 T.	olive oil
4	cloves garlic, finely minced
2 T.	fresh parsley, finely minced
1 t.	ground oregano
¼ c.	Parmesan cheese, grated
1 t.	black pepper, coarsely ground
½ t.	salt
10 oz.	angel hair pasta, hot, cooked
	nonfat cooking spray

Slice the turkey breast thinly across the grain of the meat. In a small bowl, combine the oil, garlic, parsley, oregano, Parmesan cheese, pepper and salt. Coat the grill with cooking spray and grill the turkey slices for 3–4 minutes or until fully cooked. Place the pasta on a serving platter, pour the sauce over and toss well. Arrange the turkey slices on top and serve immediately. Serves 4.

NUTRITIONAL ANALYSIS: Calories: 349 Total fat: 13 g Saturated fat: 3 g
% calories from fat: 34 Carbohydrates: 20 g Protein: 36 g Cholesterol: 110 mg Sodium: 871 mg

Orange Ginger Grilled Chicken

A piquant sauce!

½ c.	concentrated frozen orange juice
1 t.	ground ginger
¼ c.	orange marmalade
2 T.	water
1 t.	salt
½ t.	black pepper
4	boneless, skinless chicken breast halves
1	naval orange, peeled and cut into thin slices
	nonfat cooking spray

Coat the grill with cooking spray and preheat for 5 minutes. In a small bowl, combine the juice, ginger, marmalade, water, salt and pepper. Mix well to dissolve the orange juice and marmalade. Place the chicken in the grill and cover with the sauce. Grill the chicken breasts for 5–7 minutes. To serve, garnish the chicken with the orange slices and pass the melted sauce, if desired. Serves 4.

NUTRITIONAL ANALYSIS: Calories: 294 Total fat: 6 g Saturated fat: 1 g
% calories from fat: 18 Carbohydrates: 52 g Protein: 29 g Cholesterol: 73 mg Sodium: 654 mg

Sage-Stuffed Chicken Breasts

A new twist on an old favorite.

4	boneless, skinless chicken breast halves
1 c.	prepared herb stuffing mix, cooled
2 T.	onion, finely chopped
1 t.	ground sage
½ t.	dried rosemary
	nonfat cooking spray

Place the chicken on a clean cutting surface. With the tip of a sharp knife, slit each breast open without cutting through the entire breast, to create a pocket. In a medium bowl, toss together the stuffing mix, onion, sage, and rosemary. Stuff one-fourth of the dressing in each chicken breast and press the edges of the chicken breast together to close the pocket. A small bit of stuffing may spill out slightly during grilling, but this will not affect the outcome of the chicken. Lightly coat the grill with cooking spray and preheat for 5 minutes. Grill the stuffed chicken for 7–9 minutes, or until the chicken is fully cooked and the stuffing is warm. Scoop up any excess stuffing with the plastic spatula and serve with the chicken. Serves 4.

NUTRITIONAL ANALYSIS: Calories: 416 Total fat: 13 g Saturated fat: 3 g
% calories from fat: 29 Carbohydrates: 14 g Protein: 58 g Cholesterol: 146 mg Sodium: 387 mg

Chicken & Sausage Mixed Grill

Choose your favorite lowfat sausage for this tasty combination!

1	red pepper, seeded and thinly sliced
1	green pepper, seeded and thinly sliced
1	small onion, thinly sliced
1 t.	black pepper
1 t.	salt
1 T.	olive oil
1 T.	lemon juice
1 lb.	lowfat link sausage
4	boneless, skinless chicken breast halves
	nonfat cooking spray

In a large bowl, mix together the peppers, onion, black pepper, salt, oil and lemon juice. Let stand for 10 minutes to blend the flavors. Lightly coat the grill with cooking spray and preheat for 5 minutes. Cut the chicken breasts into slices approximately the same size as the sausages. Grill the chicken and sausage together for 2 minutes. Place the pepper and onion on top and grill for an additional 5–7 minutes, or until the chicken is fully cooked and the vegetables are tender. Serves 4.

NUTRITIONAL ANALYSIS: Calories: 417 Total fat: 18 g Saturated fat: 4 g
% calories from fat: 39 Carbohydrates: 13 g Protein: 51 g Cholesterol: 153 mg Sodium: 964 mg

Tandoori Grilled Chicken

The yogurt-based marinade creates exotic, tender chicken!

1	8 oz. carton unflavored lowfat yogurt
1 T.	lemon juice
2 t.	paprika
2	cloves garlic, minced
½ t.	salt
½ t.	ground ginger
½ t.	cumin
½ t.	cayenne pepper
½ t.	cinnamon
4	boneless, skinless chicken breast halves
	nonfat cooking spray

In a small bowl, mix together the yogurt, lemon juice, paprika, garlic, salt, ginger, cumin, cayenne pepper and cinnamon. Place the chicken breasts in a shallow glass pan and pour the marinade over the pieces, turning to coat thoroughly. Cover tightly and refrigerate for 1–8 hours, turning occasionally. Coat the grill with cooking spray and preheat for 5 minutes. Grill the chicken for 5–7 minutes. Discard any unused marinade. Serves 4.

NUTRITIONAL ANALYSIS: Calories: 205 Total fat: 6 g Saturated fat: 1 g % calories from fat: 26 Carbohydrates: 7 g Protein: 30 g Cholesterol: 74 mg Sodium: 385 mg

Pineapple Honey Chicken Breasts

The fresh flavor of pineapple combines with honey to produce a superior sauce!

¼ c.	low sodium soy sauce
1 t.	ginger
1 t.	vegetable oil
1	clove garlic, minced
2 T.	honey
4	boneless, skinless chicken breast halves
4	fresh pineapple slices, ½-inch thick
	(4 canned pineapple slices may be substituted)
	nonfat cooking spray

Coat the grill with cooking spray and preheat for 5 minutes. Blend the soy sauce, ginger, oil, garlic and honey. Place the chicken in the grill and spoon the soy honey sauce over each piece. Grill for 3 minutes. The sauce will melt and run into the drip tray. Place 1 slice of pineapple on each piece of chicken and grill for 3–5 minutes. If desired, you may pour the melted sauce over the grilled chicken to serve. Serves 4.

NUTRITIONAL ANALYSIS: Calories: 239 Total fat: 7 g Saturated fat: 1 g % calories from fat: 26 Carbohydrates: 15 g Protein: 29 g Cholesterol: 73 mg Sodium: 594 mg

Chicken Yakitori Kebabs

Delectable kebabs for the entire family.

4	boneless, skinless chicken breast halves	8	cherry tomatoes
2 t.	sesame oil	2	small zucchini, cut into ½-inch pieces
2	green onions, finely chopped	8	10-inch wooden skewers, soaked in water and drained
¼ c.	low sodium soy sauce		salt and pepper to taste
2 T.	brown sugar		nonfat cooking spray
2	cloves garlic, finely minced		

Cut the chicken into 1-inch cubes and place in a flat glass pan. Combine the oil, onions, soy sauce, sugar and garlic and toss with the chicken. Cover and refrigerate for 1 hour. To assemble the kebabs, thread the chicken, tomatoes and zucchini onto the skewers alternately. If desired, sprinkle the kebabs with additional salt and pepper. Lightly coat the grill with cooking spray and preheat for 5 minutes. Grill the skewers widthwise (horizontally) for 7–8 minutes or until chicken is fully cooked and zucchini is tender. Serves 4.

NUTRITIONAL ANALYSIS: Calories: 236 Total fat: 8 g Saturated fat: 1 g % calories from fat: 32 Carbohydrates: 10 g Protein: 30 g Cholesterol: 73 mg Sodium: 599 mg

Turkey Pesto Pappardelle

*Pappardelle are fun, curly-edged noodles. If you can't find them,
you may substitute fettuccine or any other long pasta.*

1	10 oz. package frozen spinach, thawed
½ c.	fresh basil leaves, packed
2 T.	olive oil
2 T.	lemon juice
2	cloves garlic, finely minced
2 lbs.	boneless, skinless turkey breast
12 oz.	pappardelle noodles, cooked
4 oz.	Parmesan cheese
4 oz.	pine nuts
	nonfat cooking spray

Press as much liquid as possible from the spinach. Assemble the spinach, basil, oil, lemon juice and garlic and chop in a food processor until the mixture is well blended and smooth to create the pesto sauce. Cut the turkey into slices approximately one-half inch thick. Coat the grill with cooking spray and preheat for 5 minutes. Grill the turkey, in batches if necessary, for 5–7 minutes, or until fully cooked. In the meantime, toss the pesto with the noodles and divide evenly among 6 dinner plates. Add the cooked turkey slices on top and sprinkle with the Parmesan cheese and pine nuts. Serves 6.

NUTRITIONAL ANALYSIS: Calories: 567 Total fat: 27 g Saturated fat: 8 g
% calories from fat: 44 Carbohydrates: 24 g Protein: 51 g Cholesterol: 123 mg Sodium: 477 mg

Yucatan Chicken Salsa

Accent this colorful meal with a fresh green salad.

4	boneless, skinless chicken breast halves
½ c.	lime juice
1 t.	black pepper
1 t.	chili powder
1 T.	olive oil
1 c.	frozen corn kernels, thawed
1	tomato, seeded and chopped
¼ c.	purple onion, chopped
1 T.	lime juice
½ t.	ground cumin
4 c.	baked lowfat tortilla chips
	nonfat cooking spray

Cut the chicken breasts into 1-inch pieces and place in a medium bowl. Combine the ½ cup lime juice, pepper, chili powder and oil and pour over the chicken. Toss to blend. In a medium bowl, mix the corn, tomato, onion, remaining lime juice and cumin to create the salsa. Coat the grill with cooking spray and preheat for 5 minutes. Grill the chicken for 5–7 minutes, or until fully cooked. Add the grilled chicken to the salsa and toss again. To serve, divide the tortilla chips among 4 individual plates and top with the chicken salsa. Serves 4.

NUTRITIONAL ANALYSIS: Calories: 206   Total fat: 7g   Saturated fat: 1g
% calories from fat: 25   Carbohydrates: 89 g   Protein: 15 g   Cholesterol: 73 mg   Sodium: 413 mg

Herbed Chicken & Mushroom Kebabs

Marinate the chicken and mushrooms at least 4 hours to absorb the mild herbs.

4	boneless, skinless chicken breast halves
1 lb.	fresh whole mushrooms, cleaned and stems removed
1 t.	dried rosemary
1 T.	dried parsley
½ t.	dried thyme
¼ c.	lemon juice
2 T.	white vinegar
½ c.	nonfat chicken broth
1 t.	black pepper
½ t.	salt
8	10-inch wooden skewers, soaked in water and drained nonfat cooking spray

Cut the chicken into 1-inch pieces and place in a medium bowl. Add the mushrooms. Combine the rosemary, parsley, thyme, juice, vinegar, broth, pepper and salt and pour over the chicken and mushrooms. Toss well. Marinate 4–12 hours in the refrigerator. Lightly coat the grill with cooking spray and preheat for 5 minutes. To assemble the kebabs, thread the chicken and mushrooms on the skewers and discard the marinade. Grill the kebabs widthwise (horizontally) for 5–7 minutes, or until the chicken is fully cooked and the mushrooms are lightly charred. Serves 4.

NUTRITIONAL ANALYSIS: Calories: 210 Total fat: 6 g Saturated fat: 1 g
% calories from fat: 26 Carbohydrates: 8 g Protein: 31 g Cholesterol: 73 mg Sodium: 379 mg

CHAPTER 7

Quick & Easy Favorites— Burgers, Sandwiches & Snacks

Burgers, sandwiches and snacks have never been so easy to prepare and fun to eat as they are when grilled in the *George Foreman Grilling Machine*! As the recipes in this chapter demonstrate, you won't be bored with healthy burger choices such as Hearty Tex-Mex Burgers, Stuffed Green Chile Burgers and Pineapple Teriyaki Burgers. We've included recipes using ground beef, pork, chicken and turkey for variety and many types of sauces and ingredients to accompany them.

Try them all—you'll soon find new family favorites!

For an exciting change of pace, try grilling any of the sandwiches or snacks from our recipe collection. Mediterranean Vegetable Sandwiches, Grilled Crab Lettuce Roll-Ups, and Poor Boy Steak Sandwiches are just a few of the delicious, lowfat sandwiches you can create. And, when you're ready to grill some very special snacks, we suggest our Salami Supreme Calzone, Grilled Won Ton or Thai Beef Satay.

Independence Day Burgers

A lowfat variation of one of our all-time favorites!

1 lb.	extra lean ground round
1 T.	Worcestershire sauce
1 t.	black pepper
1 t.	seasoned salt
1	purple onion
4	whole grain hamburger buns
	nonfat cooking spray

In a medium bowl, mix the beef, Worcestershire sauce, pepper and salt and shape into 4 hamburger patties. Slice the onion into ½-inch thick slices, being careful not to separate the rings. Lightly coat the grill with cooking spray and preheat for 5 minutes.

Place the hamburgers in the grill and cook for 4 minutes. Top each with one full slice of onion and grill for 3–4 minutes, or according to your preference. Serve the hamburgers on the buns and pass the condiments of your choice. Serves 4.

NUTRITIONAL ANALYSIS: Calories: 234 Total fat: 11 g Saturated fat: 4 g % calories from fat: 47 Carbohydrates: 4 g Protein: 24 g Cholesterol: 41 mg Sodium: 472 mg

Cheesy Beef Burgers

A favorite with children.

1 lb.	lean ground chuck
1 c.	lowfat cheddar cheese, shredded
1 T.	green onion, chopped
1 t.	salt
½ t.	black pepper
½ t.	garlic powder
1 T.	Worcestershire sauce
4	sourdough hamburger buns, split
	nonfat cooking spray

Mix together the beef, cheese, onion, salt, pepper, garlic powder and Worcestershire sauce and shape into 4 hamburger patties. Lightly coat the grill with the cooking spray and preheat for 5 minutes. Grill the hamburgers for 7–8 minutes, or according to your preference. To serve, place each burger on a sourdough bun and pass condiments of your choice. Serves 4.

NUTRITIONAL ANALYSIS: Calories: 484   Total fat: 16 g   Saturated fat: 6 g
% calories from fat: 30   Carbohydrates: 30 g   Protein: 52 g   Cholesterol: 121 mg   Sodium: 1,190 mg

Hearty Tex-Mex Burgers

These are for the biggest appetites in the house!

2 lbs.	extra lean ground round
¼ c.	prepared barbeque sauce
¼ c.	onion, finely chopped
2 T.	fresh (or bottled) salsa
1 t.	chili powder
4	extra large hamburger buns
	nonfat cooking spray

In a large bowl, thoroughly mix the beef, barbeque sauce, onion, salsa and chili powder. Shape into 4 large ¾-inch thick patties—these will be large! Lightly coat the grill with cooking spray and preheat for 5 minutes.

Grill the hamburgers for 8–9 minutes, or until cooked according to your preference. Serve the hamburgers on the buns and pass condiments of your choice. Serves 4.

NUTRITIONAL ANALYSIS: Calories: 714   Total fat: 26 g   Saturated fat: 9 g
% calories from fat: 38   Carbohydrates: 48 g   Protein: 50 g   Cholesterol: 83 mg   Sodium: 441 mg

Italiano Beef & Mozzarella Burgers

Serve open-faced on hearty peasant bread.

1 lb.	lean ground chuck
1 t.	oregano
1 t.	dried Italian seasoning
1	egg white
1	clove garlic, finely minced
2 T.	lowfat margarine
4	slices peasant bread, ½-inch thick, lightly toasted
4	lettuce leaves
1	tomato, thinly sliced
4	slices part-skim Mozzarella cheese
4	purple onion slices
¼ c.	lowfat Italian salad dressing

Mix together the beef, oregano, Italian seasoning, egg white and garlic. Shape into 4 patties. Preheat the grill for 5 minutes. Place the patties in the grill and cook for 7–8 minutes. Spread the margarine on the bread and top each with the lettuce, tomato, cheese and onion. Drizzle the Italian salad dressing over all. Place the cooked hamburger patties on top and serve. Serves 4.

NUTRITIONAL ANALYSIS: Calories: 424 Total fat: 15 g Saturated fat: 6 g
% calories from fat: 33 Carbohydrates: 19 g Protein: 49 g Cholesterol: 132 mg Sodium: 432 mg

Barbequed Cowboy Burgers

A homemade barbeque sauce makes these tasty!

½ c.	tomato sauce
3 T.	chopped onion
1	clove garlic, finely minced
1 T.	prepared mustard
2 T.	Worcestershire sauce
1 T.	brown sugar
1 lb.	extra lean ground round
4	whole grain hamburger buns
	nonfat cooking spray

In a small saucepan, simmer together the tomato sauce, onion, garlic, mustard, Worcestershire sauce and brown sugar. Simmer for 10 minutes and cool completely. Mix the beef with the barbeque sauce in a large bowl. Shape into 4 patties and refrigerate at least 1 hour. Lightly coat the grill with nonfat cooking spray and preheat for 5 minutes. Grill the hamburgers for 7–8 minutes. Serve on the hamburger buns with condiments of your choice. Serves 4.

NUTRITIONAL ANALYSIS: Calories: 507 Total fat: 21 g Saturated fat: 5 g % calories from fat: 38 Carbohydrates: 49 g Protein: 27 g Cholesterol: 41 mg Sodium: 411 mg

Sautéed Mushroom Burgers

Good enough for guests!

½ lb.	fresh mushrooms, cleaned and stems removed
1 t.	black pepper
1 t.	seasoned salt
½ c.	nonfat beef broth
2 T.	lowfat margarine
1 lb.	lean ground chuck
8	slices sweet French bread, ½-inch thick, toasted

Thinly slice the mushrooms into a sauté pan. Add the pepper, salt, broth and margarine and heat. Simmer until the mushrooms are tender and the sauce is slightly condensed. Preheat the grill for 5 minutes. Shape the beef into 4 patties and grill for 7–8 minutes, or according to your preference. Place 2 slices of bread on each plate and put a hamburger patty on one piece of the bread. Divide the sautéed mushrooms evenly over each hamburger and spoon additional sauce over each. Top with the second piece of bread. Serves 4.

NUTRITIONAL ANALYSIS: Calories: 393 Total fat: 10 g Saturated fat: 3 g
% calories from fat: 23 Carbohydrates: 29 g Protein: 43 g Cholesterol: 115 mg Sodium: 865 mg

Cheddar & Horseradish Beef Burgers

Zesty and bold!

1 lb.	extra lean ground round
½ c.	lowfat cheddar cheese, grated
2 T.	cream-style horseradish
½ t.	black pepper
½ t.	salt
½ t.	garlic powder
4	onion rolls, toasted and split
	nonfat cooking spray

In a medium bowl, combine the beef, cheese, horseradish, pepper, salt and garlic powder. Shape into 4 patties. Coat the grill with cooking spray and preheat for 5 minutes. Grill the burgers for 7–8 minutes and place on the onion rolls. Accompany with the condiments of your choice. Serves 4.

NUTRITIONAL ANALYSIS: Calories: 428 Total fat: 14 g Saturated fat: 5 g
% calories from fat: 30 Carbohydrates: 27 g Protein: 46 g Cholesterol: 118 mg Sodium: 747 mg

Stuffed Green Chile Burgers

A favorite from sunny Arizona!

1 lb.	lean ground chuck
4	whole mild green chiles, canned
¼ c.	salsa (fresh or canned)
1 t.	black pepper
4	slices lowfat Pepper Jack cheese
4	flour tortillas, warmed

Divide the beef into 4 portions. Divide each portion in half again and shape into thin patties. On top of 4 patties, place 1 green chile and 1 tablespoon of salsa. Sprinkle with black pepper and top with another beef patty, sealing the edges completely.

Preheat the grill for 5 minutes. Grill the stuffed burgers for 7–8 minutes, or according to your preference. Place each patty on 1 tortilla, top with 1 slice of the cheese and add condiments of your choice. Serves 4.

NUTRITIONAL ANALYSIS: Calories: 459 Total fat: 16 g Saturated fat: 7 g
% calories from fat: 32 Carbohydrates: 27 g Protein: 50 g Cholesterol: 135 mg Sodium: 641 mg

Ranchero Burgers

Made with beef, beans, and spices, these are surprisingly good—and good for you!

3/4 lb.	extra lean ground round
1/2 c.	canned kidney beans, drained and mashed
2	cloves garlic, minced
1/4 c.	prepared barbeque sauce
1/2 t.	salt
1/2 t.	black pepper
4	sesame seeded hamburger buns
	nonfat cooking spray

Mix together thoroughly the beef, beans, garlic, barbeque sauce, salt and pepper. Shape into 4 patties. Lightly coat the grill with the cooking spray and preheat for 5 minutes. Grill the hamburgers for 7–8 minutes, or according to your preference. Place each on a sesame bun and serve with your choice of condiments. Serves 4.

NUTRITIONAL ANALYSIS: Calories: 502 Total fat: 19 g Saturated fat: 4 g
% calories from fat: 35 Carbohydrates: 57 g Protein: 23 g Cholesterol: 31 mg Sodium: 663 mg

Asian Chicken Burgers

Lowfat and delicious!

1 lb.	lean ground chicken
1 T.	lemon juice
1	clove garlic, minced
2	green onions, finely chopped
2 T.	low sodium soy sauce
½ t.	ginger
1	egg white
4	sesame seeded hamburger buns
	nonfat cooking spray

In a large bowl, combine the chicken, lemon juice, garlic, green onions, soy sauce, ginger and egg white. Shape into 4 patties. Refrigerate for 1 hour. Coat the grill with cooking spray and preheat for 5 minutes. Grill the patties for 7–8 minutes, or according to your preference. Serve on the sesame seed buns and pass condiments such as lowfat peanut butter, hoisin sauce and bean sprouts. Serves 4.

NUTRITIONAL ANALYSIS: Calories: 721 Total fat: 16 g Saturated fat: >1 g
% calories from fat: 19 Carbohydrates: 138 g Protein: 16 g Cholesterol: 0 mg Sodium: 823 mg

Ranch Style Chicken Burgers

These burgers are chock full of surprising ingredients.

1 lb.	lean ground chicken
¼ t.	garlic powder
½ t.	Tabasco sauce
¼ t.	seasoned salt
½ t.	black pepper, coarsely ground
1 T.	fresh cilantro, finely minced
2 T.	diced green chile peppers, canned
2 T.	nonfat ranch salad dressing
4	hamburger buns
	nonfat cooking spray

Mix together the chicken, garlic powder, salt, pepper, cilantro, chile peppers and salad dressing. Shape into 4 patties. Coat the grill with cooking spray and preheat for 5 minutes.

Grill the patties for 7–8 minutes, or according to your preference. Place each patty on a bun and serve with condiments of your choice. Serves 4.

NUTRITIONAL ANALYSIS: Calories: 567   Total fat: 17 g   Saturated fat: >1 g   % calories from fat: 19   Carbohydrates: 93 g   Protein: 17 g   Cholesterol: 0 mg   Sodium: 1,213 mg

Pineapple Teriyaki Burgers

Full of flavor, not fat!

1 lb.	lean ground chicken
1	egg white
¼ c.	bottled teriyaki sauce
¼ c.	onion, chopped
½ t.	black pepper
1 t.	prepared mustard
4	slices fresh pineapple, ¼-inch thick (or 4 canned slices, if desired)
4	sesame seed hamburger buns nonfat cooking spray

Combine the chicken, egg white, teriyaki sauce, onion, pepper and mustard in a medium bowl. Shape into 4 patties. Lightly coat the grill with cooking spray and preheat for 5 minutes. Grill the patties for 3 minutes. Open the grill and add 1 slice of pineapple to each patty. Grill for 4–5 minutes, or according to your preference. Serve on sesame seed hamburger buns or over steamed brown rice. Serves 4.

NUTRITIONAL ANALYSIS: Calories: 749 Total fat: 16 g Saturated fat: >1 g % calories from fat: 18 Carbohydrates: 144 g Protein: 17 g Cholesterol: 0 mg Sodium: 1,263 mg

Down Home Turkey Burgers

Savor the hickory-smoked, barbequed flavor.

1 lb.	lean ground turkey
2 T.	liquid smoke
1	egg white
1	clove garlic, minced
2 T.	hickory-flavored barbeque sauce
2 T.	onion, finely chopped
¼ c.	fresh bread crumbs
1 t.	salt
½ t.	black pepper
4	whole grain hamburger buns
	nonfat cooking spray

Mix together the turkey, liquid smoke, egg white, garlic, barbeque sauce, onion, bread crumbs, salt and pepper. Shape into 4 patties. Lightly coat the grill with cooking spray and preheat for 5 minutes. Grill the turkey burgers for 7–8 minutes, or according to your preference. Place each patty on a hamburger bun and pass with your choice of accompaniments. Serves 4.

NUTRITIONAL ANALYSIS: Calories: 448   Total fat: 20 g   Saturated fat: 3 g
% calories from fat: 36   Carbohydrates: 50 g   Protein: 27 g   Cholesterol: 64 mg   Sodium: 837 mg

Swiss Turkey Burgers

The cheese adds a delectable flavor!

1 lb.	lean ground turkey
6 oz.	lowfat Swiss cheese, shredded
1	egg white
1 T.	Dijon mustard
¼ c.	fresh bread crumbs
1 t.	black pepper
1 t.	seasoned salt
4	onion rolls, split
	nonfat cooking spray

Combine the turkey, Swiss cheese, egg white, mustard, bread crumbs, pepper and salt in a medium bowl. Shape into 4 patties. Lightly coat the grill with cooking spray and preheat for 5 minutes. Grill the burgers for 7–8 minutes, or according to your preference. Place each burger in a bun and serve with condiments of your choice. Serves 4.

NUTRITIONAL ANALYSIS: Calories: 409   Total fat: 13 g   Saturated fat: 5 g
% calories from fat: 27   Carbohydrates: 34 g   Protein: 41 g   Cholesterol: 79 mg   Sodium: 958 mg

Turkey Burgers with Cranberry Glaze

Enjoy the essence of turkey and cranberry!

1 lb.	lean ground turkey
1	egg white
1 T.	Worcestershire sauce
1	clove garlic, minced
1 t.	black pepper
½ c.	jellied cranberry sauce, canned
1 t.	lemon juice
4	whole wheat hamburger buns, split
4	romaine lettuce leaves
¼ c.	walnuts, finely chopped
	nonfat cooking spray

Lightly coat the grill with cooking spray and preheat for 5 minutes. Combine the turkey, egg white, Worcestershire sauce, garlic and pepper and shape into 4 burgers. Combine the cranberry sauce and lemon juice in a small saucepan and heat until it is smooth. Place the turkey patties in the grill and smooth 1 tablespoon of the glaze over each. Grill for 4 minutes. Open the grill and spoon sauce over each patty again. Grill 3–4 minutes. To serve, place the buns on individual plates. Put one lettuce leaf on one half of the bun, place the turkey burger over that, spoon additional sauce over the patty and sprinkle chopped walnuts over all. Serves 4.

NUTRITIONAL ANALYSIS: Calories: 513 Total fat: 24 g Saturated fat: 3 g % calories from fat: 38 Carbohydrates: 57 g Protein: 28 g Cholesterol: 64 mg Sodium: 173 mg

Dijon Pork Burgers

The lean pork combines with mustard to create a special burger!

1 lb.	lean ground pork
2 T.	Dijon mustard
2 T.	nonfat mayonnaise
2 T.	onion, chopped
1 t.	black pepper
½ t.	salt
4	Kaiser rolls, split
	nonfat cooking spray

Combine the pork, mustard, mayonnaise, onion, pepper and salt. Shape into 4 burgers. Coat the grill with cooking spray and preheat for 5 minutes. Grill the patties for 7–8 minutes, or until fully cooked. Serve on Kaiser rolls with condiments of your choice. Serves 4.

NUTRITIONAL ANALYSIS: Calories: 364 Total fat: 15 g Saturated fat: 3 g
% calories from fat: 37 Carbohydrates: 30 g Protein: 26 g Cholesterol: 32 mg Sodium: 869 mg

Mediterranean Lamb Burgers

Try this for an exotic twist on hamburgers!

1 lb.	lean ground lamb
½ t.	black pepper, coarsely ground
½ t.	dried rosemary
½ t.	salt
2 T.	purple onion, chopped
1 T.	lemon juice
1 T.	prepared mustard
	nonfat cooking spray
4	soft pitas (or hamburger buns, if desired)
	sliced purple onions
	lettuce leaves
	sliced cucumber
	sliced tomatoes

Combine the lamb, pepper, rosemary, salt, onion, juice and mustard in a medium bowl. Shape into 4 patties. Coat the grill with cooking spray and preheat for 5 minutes. Grill the patties for 6–7 minutes, or until fully cooked. Serve in the pita pockets and pass the onions, lettuce, cucumber and tomatoes as condiments. Serves 4.

NUTRITIONAL ANALYSIS: Calories: 443 Total fat: 20 g Saturated fat: 7 g % calories from fat: 40 Carbohydrates: 42 g Protein: 27 g Cholesterol: 75 mg Sodium: 747 mg

Santa Fe Veggie Burgers

These "meatless" burgers are very satisfying.

1 c.	steamed white rice, cooked and cooled
½ c.	corn kernels, canned
1	green pepper, seeded and finely chopped
½ c.	white onion, finely chopped
1 t.	black pepper, coarsely ground
1 t.	salt
1 t.	lemon juice
1 t.	chili powder
4	whole grain hamburger buns
	nonfat cooking spray

In the bowl of a food processor, combine the rice, corn, green pepper, onion, pepper, salt, juice and chili powder. Pulse rapidly to produce a coarse, mealy texture. Shape the vegetable-rice mixture into 4 patties and refrigerate for 2 hours. Lightly coat the grill with cooking spray and preheat for 5 minutes. Grill the patties for 6–7 minutes, or until well-browned. Place the patties in the hamburger buns and top with your choice of accompaniments. Serves 4.

NUTRITIONAL ANALYSIS: Calories: 357   Total fat: 13 g   Saturated fat: >1 g
% calories from fat: 32   Carbohydrates: 58 g   Protein: 5 g   Cholesterol: 0 mg   Sodium: 64 mg

Portabella Mushroom Burgers

A meatless burger with a fresh, savory flavor.

4	Portabella mushrooms, cleaned and stems removed
2 T.	olive oil
2 T.	balsamic vinegar
2	cloves garlic, finely minced
1 T.	Italian seasoning
1 t.	black pepper, coarsely ground
4	Kaiser rolls, split
	nonfat cooking spray

Lightly coat the grill with cooking spray and preheat for 5 minutes. Place the mushrooms in the grill, underside facing up. Drizzle the oil and vinegar over each mushroom and sprinkle with the garlic, Italian seasoning and pepper. Grill for 5–6 minutes, or until tender. Serve in Kaiser rolls and pass condiments such as sliced onion, lowfat Mozzarella cheese, tomato, etc. Serves 4.

NUTRITIONAL ANALYSIS: Calories: 256 Total fat: 13 g Saturated fat: 3 g % calories from fat: 44 Carbohydrates: 31 g Protein: 6 g Cholesterol: 0 mg Sodium: 312 mg

SANDWICHES & SNACKS

Hot Sausage Sandwiches

Perfect for supper!

1 lb.	lowfat hot Italian sausage links
1	tomato, sliced
1	green pepper, seeded and thinly sliced
1	small purple onion, thinly sliced
1	clove garlic, finely minced
1 t.	black pepper, coarsely ground
1 t.	dried Italian seasoning
¼ c.	nonfat mayonnaise
4	hero sandwich buns, split and toasted
	nonfat cooking spray

Coat the grill with cooking spray and preheat for 5 minutes. On the grill, arrange the sausages widthwise (horizontally) and place the tomato, green pepper and onion around the links. Mix together the garlic, black pepper and Italian seasoning and sprinkle over the sausage-vegetable mixture. Grill for 6–7 minutes, or until heated through completely. Lightly spread the mayonnaise on each split bun and pile the sausage vegetable mixture inside. Serves 4.

NUTRITIONAL ANALYSIS: Calories: 469 Total fat: 17 g Saturated fat: 5 g
% calories from fat: 31 Carbohydrates: 49 g Protein: 31 g Cholesterol: 80 mg Sodium: 798 mg

Salami Supreme Calzone

Grilled Calzone? You won't believe it until you try these delicious sandwich pockets!

Calzone Crust:

¼ oz.	active dry yeast
⅔ c.	warm water (110°–115°)
1 t.	salt
1 T.	sugar
¼ c.	vegetable oil
2 c.	all-purpose flour

Calzone Filling:

6 T.	tomato sauce
1	clove garlic, finely minced
1 T.	fresh parsley, finely minced
1 t.	Italian seasoning
½ t.	ground oregano
1 t.	black pepper
16	slices lowfat salami
½ c.	green pepper, seeded, finely chopped
½ c.	onion, finely chopped
1 c.	lowfat Mozzarella cheese, shredded
	nonfat cooking spray

To prepare the calzone crust, completely dissolve the yeast in the warm water in a large bowl. Stir well. Add the salt, sugar and oil. Blend again. Add the flour, 1 cup at a time, mixing until the dough can be shaped into a ball with your hands. Turn the dough onto a floured board and knead gently for 3 minutes. Lightly coat a clean bowl with cooking spray and place the dough in the bowl. Turn the dough, cover and let rise for 1 hour. Punch down and let rise for 45 minutes. Divide the dough in half. On a lightly floured board, roll out each half to a circle about 8 inches in diameter and ⅛-inch thick.

To assemble, lightly coat the grill with cooking spray and preheat for 5 minutes. On one half of each dough circle, spoon the tomato sauce over the dough. Add garlic, parsley, Italian seasoning, oregano and black pepper. Top each half with salami, green pepper, onion and Mozzarella cheese. Fold each remaining half circle of dough over the toppings and press the edges together to form a tight seal. Using a large spatula, place one calzone in the grill and cook for 5–6 minutes, or until the crust is browned and the filling is hot. Remove from the grill and repeat with the remaining calzone. Makes 2 calzone, enough for 4 servings.

NUTRITIONAL ANALYSIS: Calories: 621   Total fat: 24 g   Saturated fat: 10 g   % calories from fat: 36   Carbohydrates: 67 g   Protein: 29 g   Cholesterol: 36 mg   Sodium: 2,398 mg

Poor Boy Steak Sandwiches

For any day of the week.

1 lb.	chuck steak
1 t.	black pepper
½ t.	salt
1	4 oz. can diced green chiles
1	small tomato, diced
1 T.	Dijon mustard
1 T.	nonfat mayonnaise
4	large hero-style sandwich buns, split and toasted

Preheat the grill for 5 minutes. Remove any visible fat from the steak and slice the steak in thin strips across the grain of the meat. Place in the grill and sprinkle with pepper and salt. Grill for 2–3 minutes. Add the green chiles and tomato. Grill for 2 minutes. Spread the Dijon mustard on one side of each bun and mayonnaise on the other. Pack the meat mixture inside each hero and serve with onions, if desired. Serves 4.

NUTRITIONAL ANALYSIS: Calories: 445 Total fat: 12 g Saturated fat: 5 g
% calories from fat: 25 Carbohydrates: 36 g Protein: 45 g Cholesterol: 114 mg Sodium: 945 mg

Grilled Garden Vegetable Sandwiches

A healthy alternative to high-fat lunches.

2	zucchini, thinly sliced
½	small purple onion, thinly sliced
1	red pepper, seeded and thinly sliced
10	mushrooms, thinly sliced
1 c.	eggplant, diced
1 T.	olive oil
1	clove garlic, finely minced
1 t.	black pepper, coarsely ground
½ t.	salt
4	onion rolls, split and toasted
¼ c.	lowfat Parmesan cheese, grated
	nonfat cooking spray

Lightly coat the grill with cooking spray and preheat for 5 minutes. Layer the zucchini, onion, red pepper, mushrooms and eggplant in the grill and sprinkle the oil, garlic, pepper and salt over the vegetables. Grill for 5–6 minutes. Top each roll with equal portions of the vegetables and sprinkle Parmesan cheese over each sandwich. Serves 4.

NUTRITIONAL ANALYSIS: Calories: 262 Total fat: 10 g Saturated fat: 2 g
% calories from fat: 32 Carbohydrates: 35 g Protein: 11 g Cholesterol: 5 mg Sodium: 680 mg

Grilled Crab Lettuce Roll-ups

These are delicate and perfect for a light luncheon.

12 oz.	fresh crabmeat, or 12 oz. canned crabmeat, drained
1 c.	fresh bread crumbs (white or whole wheat)
½ c.	onion, finely chopped
½ c.	nonfat mayonnaise
1 T.	Dijon mustard
½ t.	black pepper
½ t.	salt
8	large romaine or butter lettuce leaves, cleaned and drained
¼ c.	prepared crab cocktail sauce nonfat cooking spray

Coat the grill with cooking spray and preheat for 5 minutes. Combine the crabmeat, bread crumbs, onion, mayonnaise, mustard, pepper and salt. Lightly spread the mixture in the grill and cook for 2–3 minutes. The crab mixture will be heated through and lightly browned when done. With the plastic spatula, remove the crab filling from the grill and place on 4 individual plates. To assemble, place a heaping spoonful of crab on each lettuce leaf and roll up. Dip the lettuce into the cocktail sauce, as desired. Makes 8 roll-ups, enough for 4 servings.

NUTRITIONAL ANALYSIS: Calories: 269 Total fat: 3 g Saturated fat: >1 g % calories from fat: 11 Carbohydrates: 32 g Protein: 23 g Cholesterol: 60 mg Sodium: 1,228 mg

Grilled Ahi Tuna Sandwiches

A sophisticated sandwich for lunch or dinner.
Grill the tuna to rare or medium-rare for best results.

1 t.	ground ginger
1 T.	low sodium soy sauce
1 t.	garlic powder
1 T.	lemon juice
4	4 oz. ahi tuna steaks
¼ c.	nonfat mayonnaise
4	4-inch French bread rolls
	fresh lettuce leaves
1	small tomato, thinly sliced
	nonfat cooking spray

In a small bowl, combine the ginger, soy sauce, garlic powder and lemon juice. Lightly coat the grill with cooking spray and preheat for 5 minutes. Place the tuna in the grill and spoon the ginger soy sauce over each piece. Grill for 4–7 minutes, or according to your preference. Lightly spread the mayonnaise on the French bread rolls, layer with the lettuce and tomato and place the grilled tuna on top. Serves 4.

NUTRITIONAL ANALYSIS: Calories: 294 Total fat: 6 g Saturated fat: >1 g % calories from fat: 18 Carbohydrates: 25 g Protein: 39 g Cholesterol: 66 mg Sodium: 704 mg

Chicken Cheese Quesadillas

A simple "quick-fix" for any time of the day.

1	chicken breast, boned and skinned
4	flour tortillas
1 c.	lowfat cheddar cheese
2 T.	green onion, chopped
½ c.	prepared mild tomato salsa
	nonfat cooking spray

Lightly coat the grill with cooking spray and preheat for 5 minutes. Grill the chicken breast for 5–7 minutes, or until fully cooked. Cool and chop into small pieces. Lightly coat the grill with the cooking spray again. On one half of 1 tortilla, place one-fourth of the chicken, cheese, onion and salsa. Fold the top half over the cheese and chicken and grill for 2–3 minutes, or until the quesadilla is lightly browned and the cheese is melted. Remove and repeat the grilling process with the remaining tortillas. Serves 4.

NUTRITIONAL ANALYSIS: Calories: 342 Total fat: 11 g Saturated fat: 3 g
% calories from fat: 28 Carbohydrates: 42 g Protein: 18 g Cholesterol: 16 mg Sodium: 624 mg

Thai Beef Satay

An excellent appetizer or snack.

1½ lb.	beef top round
½ c.	low sodium soy sauce
½ t.	ground ginger
1	clove garlic, minced
1 t.	white vinegar
1	green onion, finely chopped
1 T.	honey
10	8-inch wooden skewers, soaked in water and drained
2 oz.	dry-roasted peanuts, chopped
	nonfat cooking spray

Remove any visible fat from the beef. Cut into very thin slices and place in a large resealable plastic bag. In a small serving bowl, combine the soy sauce, ginger, garlic, vinegar, green onion and honey and pour over the beef. Seal the bag, removing as much air as possible, and refrigerate for 12 hours. Lightly coat the grill with cooking spray and preheat for 5 minutes. Thread the beef slices through the skewers in an accordion fashion, adjusting the meat to uniformly fit the skewers. Discard the marinade. Grill the beef widthwise (horizontally) for 3–4 minutes, or according to your preference. Sprinkle each skewer with the chopped peanuts just before serving. Serves 10.

NUTRITIONAL ANALYSIS: Calories: 153 Total fat: 6 g Saturated fat: 2 g % calories from fat: 37 Carbohydrates: 4 g Protein: 17 g Cholesterol: 41 mg Sodium: 462 mg

Grilled Won Ton

A new twist on an Oriental favorite!

1	chicken breast, boned and skinned
¼ c.	water chestnuts, finely diced
½ c.	bean sprouts, finely chopped
1	clove garlic, finely minced
2 T.	low sodium soy sauce
¼ c.	hoisin sauce
1 T.	Szechwan chili sauce
16	won ton noodle squares
	nonfat cooking spray

Coat the grill with cooking spray and preheat for 5 minutes. Grill the chicken breast for 5–7 minutes, or until fully cooked. Cool and chop into very small pieces. In a medium bowl, combine the chicken, water chestnuts, bean sprouts, garlic, soy sauce, hoisin sauce and chili sauce. Mix well. Coat the grill with cooking spray again and preheat for 5 minutes. Lay 1 won ton square on a flat surface. Place 1 heaping tablespoon of the chicken and vegetable mixture on one-half of the square. Dab a bit of water on the edges of the noodle and fold the remaining half of the noodle over the top, forming a triangle and sealing the edges with your fingertips. Repeat with the remaining won ton noodle squares. Place 4 won ton in the grill and cook for about 5 minutes, or until browned and crisp. Repeat with the remaining won ton. Serve with additional soy sauce, if desired. Serves 8.

NUTRITIONAL ANALYSIS: Calories: 122 Total fat: 1 g Saturated fat: >1 g
% calories from fat: 11 Carbohydrates: 15 g Protein: 9 g Cholesterol: 20 mg Sodium: 382 mg

TEMPTING COMPANION DISHES— VEGETABLES, FRUIT, SALADS & DESSERTS

The *George Foreman Grilling Machine* brings out the very best of vegetables and fruit! If you can imagine tender-crisp grilled vegetables and warm, sweet grilled fruit, you'll enjoy the wide variety of recipes that follow in this chapter. From Creamy Dill Carrots and Cheesy Grilled New Potatoes to Quick & Easy Grilled Bananas and Grilled Apple Pecan Cups, you'll find vegetable and fruit dishes to satisfy every appetite! Also, because fruit is so naturally sweet, we've included recipes for fruit desserts that are quick and easy to prepare.

Vegetables are typically lowfat and naturally healthful food choices. And, grilling complements vegetables by releasing natural liquids and expanding the true flavor of the vegetables. Vegetables should be uniformly cut or sliced and they should be 1 inch or less in thickness in order to properly grill. We suggest that you coat the grill with nonfat cooking spray before heating the grill. Firm vegetables work especially well in the grill, including squash, eggplant, potatoes, Brussels sprouts and carrots. Herbs and spices with lemon or vinegar add a dash of personality to the vegetables as they grill. If you prefer, you may also marinate vegetables and then grill them for added flavor.

Fruit is, without a doubt, the most wonderful and natural salad or dessert when it is grilled to tenderness. The quick, hot grilling process seals in the fruit juice and warms the fruit very rapidly. Firm fruits such as apples, pineapple, peaches, bananas and nectarines grill nicely. Because fruit will lose its texture and become mushy when overcooked, always watch the grill carefully and check the fruit a few minutes before it's supposed to be done. Perfectly grilled fruit is tender-crisp and warm throughout. For a dessert treat, combine fruit with lowfat frozen yogurt or fat-free pudding.

Hearty salads begin on the grill. Whether you choose to grill a small sirloin steak for a large Asian noodle salad, or build a chicken Caesar salad by grilling tender chicken breast strips, you'll find that the grill is the start of unique and delicious salads. We've included in this chapter recipes for lowfat salads that give you all the flavors you love, while eliminating the heavy fat dressings and toppings.

VEGETABLES

Italian Portabella Mushrooms

Lightly grill these tender mushrooms for a fresh-roasted flavor.

4	Portabella mushrooms, cleaned, dried and stems removed
1 T.	olive oil
1 t.	balsamic vinegar
¼ t.	Italian seasoning
¼ t.	black pepper
½ t.	salt
	nonfat cooking spray

Arrange the mushrooms on a flat tray, with the undersides facing up. Mix together the oil, vinegar, Italian seasoning, pepper and salt and lightly drizzle over the mushrooms. Coat the grill with cooking spray and preheat for 5 minutes. Grill the mushrooms, undersides facing up, for 4–5 minutes. To serve, cut each mushroom into 4 wedges and arrange on a serving platter. Serves 4.

NUTRITIONAL ANALYSIS: Calories: 226 Total fat: 6 g Saturated fat: 2 g % calories from fat: 28 Carbohydrates: 31 g Protein: 6 g Cholesterol: 0 mg Sodium: 310 mg

Rosemary Brussels Sprouts

The light herb and butter flavors accentuate the bold flavors of the sprouts.

1	16 oz. package frozen Brussels sprouts, thawed and drained
½ t.	fresh rosemary, finely minced
2 T.	lowfat margarine
½ t.	garlic salt
¼ t.	black pepper
	nonfat cooking spray

Pat the sprouts dry and cut each in half. In a small bowl, mix together the rosemary, lowfat margarine, garlic salt and pepper. Coat the grill with cooking spray and preheat for 5 minutes. Place the sprouts in the grill and spread the herb butter over the sprouts. Grill the sprouts for 8–9 minutes. As the herb butter melts, it will drip into the grilling tray. To serve, spoon the sprouts into a bowl and pour the melted herb butter over them. Serves 4.

NUTRITIONAL ANALYSIS: Calories: 87 Total fat: 4 g Saturated fat: >1 g
% calories from fat: 39 Carbohydrates: 10 g Protein: 4 g Cholesterol: 0 mg Sodium: 276 mg

Grilled Winter Squash

This is super-quick and easy.

1 lb.	winter squash
2 T.	lowfat margarine
½ t.	black pepper
½ t.	seasoned salt
	nonfat cooking spray

Clean the squash and remove the seeds and woody fibers. Dice the squash into small cubes about ¼-inch square. Coat the grill with cooking spray and preheat for 5 minutes. Mix together the lowfat margarine, black pepper and salt in a small bowl. Place the squash in the grill and brush with the butter mixture. Grill for 6–8 minutes, or until tender. As the herb butter melts, it will drip into the grilling tray. To serve, place the squash in a serving bowl and pour the melted seasoned butter over the squash. Serves 4.

NUTRITIONAL ANALYSIS: Calories: 50 Total fat: 1 g Saturated fat: >1 g
% calories from fat: 24 Carbohydrates: 9 g Protein: >1 g Cholesterol: 0 mg Sodium: 213 mg

Grilled Garlic Zucchini

The mild squash flavor is accompanied by a hearty garlic spread.

3	zucchini, medium-sized
2 T.	olive oil
2 T.	lemon juice
2	cloves garlic, finely minced
¼ t.	black pepper, coarsely ground
½ t.	salt
	nonfat cooking spray

Peel the zucchini and cut lengthwise into thin matchstick pieces. Combine the oil, lemon juice, garlic, pepper and salt in a medium-sized bowl. Toss the zucchini with the garlic mixture and let stand for 10 minutes to allow the zucchini to absorb the flavors. Lightly coat the grill with cooking spray and preheat for 5 minutes. Grill the zucchini widthwise (horizontally) for 4–5 minutes, or until tender-crisp. Serves 4.

NUTRITIONAL ANALYSIS: Calories: 40 Total fat: 3 g Saturated fat: >1 g % calories from fat: 50 Carbohydrates: 4 g Protein: 2 g Cholesterol: 0 mg Sodium: 3 mg

Creamy Dill Carrots

Grilled sweet carrots smothered with a tangy sauce—delicious!

10	fresh carrots, peeled
¼ c.	fat free mayonnaise
¼ c.	fat free sour cream
1 t.	fresh dill, finely minced
½ t.	lemon juice
½ t.	black pepper
1 t.	nonfat milk
1 T.	olive oil
	nonfat cooking spray

Cut the carrots into halves lengthwise and in half widthwise. Combine the mayonnaise, sour cream, dill, lemon juice, pepper and milk in a small bowl. Blend thoroughly, cover and store in the refrigerator until ready to use. Coat the grill with cooking spray and preheat for 5 minutes. Place the carrots widthwise (horizontally) in the grill, cut side up and lightly drizzle with the oil. Grill for approximately 5–7 minutes, or until tender-crisp. To serve, place the carrots in a warmed serving dish and pass the dill sauce as an accompaniment. Serves 4.

NUTRITIONAL ANALYSIS: Calories: 137 Total fat: 4 g Saturated fat: >1 g % calories from fat: 23 Carbohydrates: 25 g Protein: 3 g Cholesterol: 1 mg Sodium: 181 mg

Zesty Marinated Zucchini

This marinade combined with the fresh zucchini makes a memorable grilled vegetable!

4	medium-sized zucchini
3 T.	olive oil
¼ c.	lemon juice
1 T.	balsamic vinegar
2	cloves garlic, finely minced
½ t.	dried basil
1 t.	black pepper
¼ t.	salt
	nonfat cooking spray

Scrub the zucchini and cut into slices ½-inch thick. In a 9" x 9" glass pan, combine the oil, lemon juice, vinegar, garlic, basil, pepper and salt. Add the zucchini and mix well. Cover with plastic wrap and refrigerate overnight.

Lightly coat the grill with cooking spray and preheat for 5 minutes. Place the zucchini in the grill, overlapping the slices, and cook for 6–8 minutes, or until tender-crisp. Serve on a warmed platter. Serves 6.

NUTRITIONAL ANALYSIS: Calories: 8 Total fat: >1 g Saturated fat: >1 g
% calories from fat: 49 Carbohydrates: >1 g Protein: >1 g Cholesterol: 0 mg Sodium: 17 mg

Italian Yellow Squash

Serve with lamb, chicken or turkey.

1 lb.	yellow squash
1 T.	parsley, finely minced
1 t.	Italian seasoning
½ t.	oregano
2 T.	olive oil
1 T.	balsamic vinegar
½ t.	black pepper
	nonfat cooking spray

Clean the squash and cut into slices ¼-inch thick. In a small bowl, mix together the parsley, Italian seasoning, oregano, olive oil, vinegar and pepper. Lightly coat the grill with cooking spray and preheat for 5 minutes.

Place the squash in the grill, overlapping the slices, and cook for 6–8 minutes. In a serving bowl, lightly toss the squash with the Italian dressing and serve immediately. Serves 4.

NUTRITIONAL ANALYSIS: Calories: 73 Total fat: 5 g Saturated fat: >1 g % calories from fat: 61 Carbohydrates: 6 g Protein: 1 g Cholesterol: 0 mg Sodium: 15 mg

Purple Onion & Sweet Red Peppers

A delicious combination!

2	sweet red peppers
1	medium purple onion
1 T.	garlic, finely minced
1 t.	black pepper
1 t.	lemon juice
	nonfat cooking spray

Clean the peppers and remove the seeds and inner fibers. Slice into rings ¼-inch thick. Remove the outer skin from the onion and slice into rings ¼-inch thick. In a medium bowl, toss the vegetables with the garlic, pepper and lemon juice. Coat the grill with cooking spray and preheat for 5 minutes. Layer the peppers and onion in the grill and cook for 6–8 minutes. Vegetables will be tender-crisp when done. Serve immediately on a warmed platter. Serves 4.

NUTRITIONAL ANALYSIS: Calories: 29 Total fat: 0 g Saturated fat: >1 g % calories from fat: 5 Carbohydrates: 7 g Protein: >1 g Cholesterol: 0 mg Sodium: >1 mg

Sicilian Grilled Eggplant

This mild vegetable pairs well with the full-flavored tomato sauce.

1	medium-sized eggplant
1 t.	black pepper
8 oz.	tomato sauce
½ c.	fresh tomato, diced
1 T.	fresh garlic, minced
1 T.	fresh parsley, minced
1 t.	black pepper
½ t.	salt
2 T.	Asiago cheese, shredded
	nonfat cooking spray

Clean, peel and cut the eggplant into ½-inch thick slices. Sprinkle with pepper. In a small saucepan, combine the tomato sauce, tomato, garlic, parsley, pepper and salt. Heat through and simmer for 10 minutes. Coat the grill with cooking spray and preheat for 5 minutes. Place the eggplant slices in the grill in a single layer and cook until tender, about 8–9 minutes. Place on a serving platter and repeat with any remaining slices. When all the eggplant slices are grilled, gently pour the tomato sauce over the slices and top with the shredded cheese. Serves 4.

NUTRITIONAL ANALYSIS: Calories: 77 Total fat: 1g Saturated fat: >1 g % calories from fat: 15 Carbohydrates: 15 g Protein: 3 g Cholesterol: 3 mg Sodium: 650 mg

Asparagus with Lemon Dill Butter

Serve warm or, in the hottest days of summertime, chilled. Either way, it's delectable!

1 lb.	fresh asparagus
⅓ c.	lowfat margarine
2 t.	lemon juice
1 t.	fresh dill, finely minced
¼ t.	salt
¼ t.	pepper
	nonfat cooking spray

Clean the asparagus and cut off the woody end pieces, if necessary, to fit inside the grill. Pat dry. In a small serving bowl, combine the margarine, lemon juice and dill. Lightly coat the grill with cooking spray and preheat for 5 minutes. Place asparagus side-by-side in the grill lengthwise (vertically) and lightly salt and pepper. Cook for 3–4 minutes, or until tender-crisp. Be careful not to burn or overcook the asparagus. Place on a warmed serving platter. To serve, place a tablespoon of the lemon butter on each serving of asparagus. Serves 4.

NUTRITIONAL ANALYSIS: Calories: 65 Total fat: 2 g Saturated fat: >1 g % calories from fat: 35 Carbohydrates: 6 g Protein: 2 g Cholesterol: 0 mg Sodium: 247 mg

Tuscan Purple Onions

Perfect with beef.

2 T.	olive oil
1 T.	balsamic vinegar
1 t.	fresh rosemary, finely minced
2 T.	fresh parsley, finely minced
½ t.	dried oregano
1 t.	black pepper
¼ t.	salt
1 lb.	purple onions
	nonfat cooking spray

In a 9" x 13" glass dish, combine the oil, vinegar, rosemary, parsley, oregano, pepper and salt. Cut the onions into slices ¼-inch thick. Do not separate the slices. Place each slice in the glass pan and turn to coat. Lightly coat the grill with cooking spray and preheat for 5 minutes. Grill the onion slices in a single layer for 5–6 minutes, or until lightly charred. Repeat with any remaining slices. Serves 6.

NUTRITIONAL ANALYSIS: Calories: 42   Total fat: 1 g   Saturated fat: >1 g
% calories from fat: 26   Carbohydrates: 7 g   Protein: >1 g   Cholesterol: 0 mg   Sodium: 101 mg

Easy Barbequed Onions

Fast enough for any night of the week.

2	sweet onions
¼ c.	prepared barbeque sauce
¼ t.	black pepper
¼ t	Tabasco sauce
	nonfat cooking spray

Remove the outer skins from the onions and trim off the ends. Slice each onion into ¼-inch thick slices. Do not separate the slices. Coat the grill with cooking spray and preheat for 5 minutes. Combine the barbeque sauce, pepper and Tabasco sauce in a small bowl. Place the onion slices in the grill and smooth 1 teaspoon of sauce over each. Grill for about 5–6 minutes, or until tender–crisp. Remove from the grill and repeat the process with the remaining onions. Serves 4.

NUTRITIONAL ANALYSIS: Calories: 46   Total fat: >1 g   Saturated fat: >1 g   % calories from fat: 2   Carbohydrates: 10 g   Protein: >1 g   Cholesterol: 0 mg   Sodium: 228 mg

Mixed Vegetable Grill

The grilling process brings out the bold flavors of these vegetables.
Serve with a simple cut of chicken or beef.

1	red pepper, seeded
1	green pepper, seeded
1	small purple onion
1	medium zucchini squash
1	carrot
2 T.	olive oil
1 T.	lemon juice
1 t.	black pepper
½ t.	salt
	nonfat cooking spray

Chop the peppers, onion, squash and carrot into ½-inch pieces. Coat the grill with cooking spray and preheat for 5 minutes. In a small bowl, combine the oil, lemon juice, pepper and salt. Place the vegetables in the grill and sprinkle with the oil and lemon seasonings. Grill for 6–8 minutes, or until vegetables are tender-crisp. Serves 4.

NUTRITIONAL ANALYSIS: Calories: 54 Total fat: 2 g Saturated fat: >1 g % calories from fat: 30 Carbohydrates: 9 g Protein: 2 g Cholesterol: 0 mg Sodium: 300 mg

Greek Vegetables with Lemon & Garlic

A subtle reminder of sun-drenched Greek Islands.

1	small eggplant
1	red pepper, seeded
1	green pepper, seeded
1	small white onion
10	mushrooms
2	cloves garlic, finely minced
2 T.	olive oil
1 T.	lemon juice
1	small tomato, chopped
1	small cucumber, peeled and chopped
	nonfat cooking spray

Clean the eggplant and peppers and chop into ½-inch thick slices. Peel the onion and cut into ¼-inch thick slices. Clean the mushrooms and slice thinly. Lightly coat the grill with cooking spray and preheat for 5 minutes. Grill the eggplant, peppers and onion for 3 minutes. Add the mushrooms and garlic and sprinkle with the olive oil and lemon juice. Grill for 5 minutes, or until vegetables are tender-crisp. Place in a serving bowl, top with the chopped tomato and cucumber and mix lightly. Serves 4.

NUTRITIONAL ANALYSIS: Calories: 95   Total fat: 2 g   Saturated fat: >1 g
% calories from fat: 20   Carbohydrates: 18 g   Protein: 3 g   Cholesterol: 0 mg   Sodium: 9 mg

Yukon Gold Potato Wedges

These potatoes are slightly sweet and partner well with chicken and turkey.

4	Yukon Gold Potatoes
1 t.	black pepper
1 t.	seasoned salt
½ t.	onion powder
	nonfat cooking spray

Scrub the potatoes and remove any blemishes. Cut each potato into 12 small wedges and place in a plastic bag. Add the pepper, salt and onion powder and shake the bag to coat the potatoes. Lightly coat the grill with the cooking spray and preheat for 5 minutes. Place the potatoes in a single layer in the grill and cook for about 7–9 minutes, or until tender. Repeat the process with any remaining wedges. Serves 4.

NUTRITIONAL ANALYSIS: Calories: 125 Total fat: >1 g Saturated fat: >1 g
% calories from fat: 1 Carbohydrates: 23 g Protein: 2 g Cholesterol: 0 mg Sodium: 361 mg

Spicy French Fries

A delicious, lowfat treat!

2	russet potatoes
1 T.	olive oil
1 t.	lemon juice
1 t.	black pepper
1 t.	seasoned salt
	nonfat cooking spray

Scrub the potatoes and remove any blemishes. Cut each potato into fries, about ½-inch thick and 4 inches in length. Sprinkle the oil and lemon juice over the fries and let stand for 5 minutes. Lightly coat the grill with the cooking spray and preheat for 5 minutes. Place the potatoes in the grill widthwise (horizontally) and sprinkle with pepper and seasoned salt. Grill for 7–9 minutes, or until tender. Serves 4.

NUTRITIONAL ANALYSIS: Calories: 96 Total fat: 2 g Saturated fat: >1 g
% calories from fat: 19 Carbohydrates: 14 g Protein: 2 g Cholesterol: 0 mg Sodium: 1,041 mg

Rosemary & Sage Potatoes

These potatoes are an elegant addition to any meal.

2	large baking potatoes
1 T.	fresh rosemary, finely minced
1 t.	dried sage
1 T.	black pepper, coarsely ground
1 t.	salt
	nonfat cooking spray

Scrub the potatoes and remove any blemishes. Cut each potato into slices about ½-inch thick. Pat dry. Lightly coat the grill with the cooking spray and preheat for 5 minutes. Place the slices in the grill in a single layer and sprinkle the rosemary, sage, pepper and salt on top. Grill for 7–9 minutes. Repeat the process with any remaining slices. Serves 4.

NUTRITIONAL ANALYSIS: Calories: 116   Total fat: >1 g   Saturated fat: >1 g
% calories from fat: 2   Carbohydrates: 27 g   Protein: 3 g   Cholesterol: 0 mg   Sodium: 590 mg

Cheesy Grilled New Potatoes

A hit with teenagers!

16	small new potatoes
¼ c.	green onions, thinly sliced
1 t.	black pepper
1 t.	garlic salt
2 T.	lowfat cheddar cheese, shredded
	nonfat cooking spray

Clean the potatoes and cut into slices ¼-inch thick. Pat dry. Lightly coat the grill with the cooking spray and pre-heat for 5 minutes. Place one half of the slices in the grill, add half of the green onions, and sprinkle with pepper and salt. Grill for 7–9 minutes. Place the grilled potatoes on a warmed serving tray and top with half of the cheese. Repeat the process with the remaining potato slices, onions, pepper, salt and cheese. Serves 4.

NUTRITIONAL ANALYSIS: Calories: 438 Total fat: >1 g Saturated fat: >1 g % calories from fat: 1 Carbohydrates: 94 g Protein: 10 g Cholesterol: >1 mg Sodium: 505 mg

Garlic-Stuffed Red Potatoes

Perfect for garlic lovers!

4	medium-sized red potatoes
5	cloves garlic, thinly sliced
½ t.	oregano
2 T.	fresh parsley, finely minced
1 t.	salt
½ t.	pepper
	nonfat cooking spray

Peel the potatoes and cut each into ¼-inch thick slices. With the tip of a very sharp knife, create a pocket in each potato slice and insert 1 slice of garlic into each pocket. Lightly coat the grill with the cooking spray and preheat for 5 minutes. Place the slices in the grill and sprinkle with the oregano, parsley, salt and pepper. Grill for 7–9 minutes or until tender. Serves 4.

NUTRITIONAL ANALYSIS: Calories: 151   Total fat: >1 g   Saturated fat: >1 g
% calories from fat: 1   Carbohydrates: 29 g   Protein: 3 g   Cholesterol: 0 mg   Sodium: 612 mg

Dijon Parsley Potatoes

A great accompaniment to pork or beef.

3	large baking potatoes
4 T.	Dijon mustard
2 T.	green onions, finely chopped
1 T.	parsley, finely minced
1 t.	black pepper
	nonfat cooking spray

Clean the potatoes and cut each into ¼-inch thick cubes. Coat the grill with cooking spray and preheat for 5 minutes. Place the potatoes in the grill and lightly coat with Dijon mustard. Sprinkle with the green onions, parsley and pepper. Grill for about 7–9 minutes, or until tender. Serves 4.

NUTRITIONAL ANALYSIS: Calories: 159   Total fat: 3 g   Saturated fat: >1 g
% calories from fat: 19   Carbohydrates: 27 g   Protein: 3 g   Cholesterol: 0 mg   Sodium: 306 mg

Grilled Red Potato Hash

For lunch, supper or a hearty snack.

2	chicken breast halves, boned and skinned
3	large red potatoes
½ c.	white onion, chopped
2 T.	lowfat margarine
1 t.	seasoned salt
½ t.	black pepper
2 T.	fresh parsley, minced
	nonfat cooking spray

Coat the grill with cooking spray and preheat for 5 minutes. Grill the chicken for 5–7 minutes, or until completely cooked. Chop into small pieces and set aside. Clean the potatoes and chop into small cubes (about ¼-inch). Lightly coat the grill with the cooking spray and add the potato cubes. Grill for 4 minutes. In a small bowl, mix the margarine, salt and pepper with the onion and cooked chicken. Add the chicken and onion mixture to the potatoes in the grill. Spread evenly across the grill. Grill for 3–4 additional minutes. When the potatoes are tender, remove the hash to a serving bowl. Garnish with the parsley and serve. Serves 4.

NUTRITIONAL ANALYSIS: Calories: 172 Total fat: 2 g Saturated fat: >1 g
% calories from fat: 10 Carbohydrates: 23 g Protein: 9 g Cholesterol: 18 mg Sodium: 639 mg

Honey Butter Sweet Potatoes

All the flavor without the fat!

3	medium sweet potatoes
½ c.	lowfat margarine
2 T.	honey
½ t.	ground cinnamon
	nonfat cooking spray

Clean the potatoes, peel and cut into slices about ¼-inch thick. In a small bowl, combine the margarine, honey and cinnamon and stir until smooth. Coat the grill with cooking spray and preheat for 5 minutes. Place the potato slices in the grill and cook for 3 minutes. Spoon the honey butter over the potatoes and grill for an additional 4–6 minutes. As the butter melts, it will run into the drip tray. Place the grilled potatoes on a serving platter and drizzle with the melted honey butter. Serves 4.

NUTRITIONAL ANALYSIS: Calories: 154 Total fat: 3 g Saturated fat: 1 g % calories from fat: 20 Carbohydrates: 27 g Protein: 1 g Cholesterol: 0 mg Sodium: 294 mg

FRUIT & DESSERTS

Grilled Cinnamon Peaches & Papaya

The lightly grilled fruit is perfect for a warm summer evening.

3	ripe peaches
1	papaya
¼ c.	lowfat margarine
½ t.	ground cinnamon
1 T.	concentrated apple juice

Pit and peel the peaches. Chop the fruit into small cubes (about ¼-inch thick). Peel and clean the papaya, remove the seeds, and chop into small cubes, as above. In a medium bowl, combine the margarine, cinnamon and apple juice and blend well. Add the peaches and papaya and toss lightly. Preheat the grill for 3 minutes. Grill the fruit for 2–3 minutes, or until the fruit is warm and lightly glazed. Serves 4.

NUTRITIONAL ANALYSIS: Calories: 94 Total fat: 2 g Saturated fat: >1 g % calories from fat: 16 Carbohydrates: 18 g Protein: 1 g Cholesterol: 0 mg Sodium: 79 mg

Grilled Apple Pecan Cups

Crunchy pecans naturally accompany sweet and crisp apples.

2	small baking apples
¼ c.	clover honey
2 T.	pecans, chopped
1 T.	brown sugar
	nonfat cooking spray

Peel, core and cut the apples in half crosswise. Inside the "cup" of each half, place a tablespoon of honey. Sprinkle 1 teaspoon of the chopped pecans into each "cup" of honey and dust the apples with the brown sugar. Coat the grill with cooking spray and preheat for 5 minutes. Place the apples in the grill and cook for 6–8 minutes, or until tender and warm. Watch carefully as the apples grill to avoid burning. Top with frozen lowfat vanilla yogurt or nonfat whipped topping, if desired. Serves 4.

NUTRITIONAL ANALYSIS: Calories: 157   Total fat: 3 g   Saturated fat: >1 g
% calories from fat: 17   Carbohydrates: 29 g   Protein: >1 g   Cholesterol: 0 mg   Sodium: 1 mg

Hawaiian Pineapple Slices

This is so versatile—serve as a salad or a dessert!

1	fresh pineapple
¼ c.	clover honey
1 t.	ground cinnamon
	nonfat cooking spray

Peel, core and slice the pineapple into ½-inch thick slices. In a small bowl, combine the honey and cinnamon. Coat the grill with cooking spray and preheat for 5 minutes. Place the slices in a single layer in the grill and drizzle the honey-cinnamon over the slices. Grill for 5–7 minutes, or until the pineapple is tender. Repeat with any remaining slices. Serves 6.

NUTRITIONAL ANALYSIS: Calories: 83 Total fat: >1 g Saturated fat: >1 g % calories from fat: 3 Carbohydrates: 22 g Protein: >1 g Cholesterol: 0 mg Sodium: 1 mg

Quick & Easy Grilled Bananas

This is just about the easiest fruit dessert you'll find.

2	ripe bananas, peeled
2 T.	sugar
½ t.	cinnamon
2 T.	walnuts, finely minced
	nonfat cooking spray

Cut the bananas in half widthwise and in half lengthwise. Lightly coat the grill with cooking spray and preheat for 5 minutes. Combine the sugar, cinnamon and walnuts in a small bowl. Place the bananas in the grill widthwise (horizontally) and spoon the cinnamon-walnuts over each slice. Grill for 3–4 minutes, or until the bananas are warm and the cinnamon-walnuts are slightly glazed. Serves 2.

NUTRITIONAL ANALYSIS: Calories: 262 Total fat: 5 g Saturated fat: >1 g % calories from fat: 18 Carbohydrates: 44 g Protein: 2 g Cholesterol: 0 mg Sodium: 13 mg

Grilled Strawberry Maple Shortcake

A lowfat dessert that is, "Oh, so yummy!"

1	lowfat pound cake, cut into 8 slices
¼ c.	maple syrup
2 c.	fresh strawberries, cleaned and sliced
1 c.	nonfat whipped cream topping
	nonfat cooking spray

Lightly coat the grill with cooking spray and preheat for 5 minutes. Place the pound cake slices in the grill and brush with the maple syrup. Grill for 3–5 minutes, until the cake is toasted and completely warm. Put the slices on individual plates, top with strawberries and cover with whipped topping.
Serves 4.

NUTRITIONAL ANALYSIS: Calories: 460 Total fat: 3 g Saturated fat: >1 g
% calories from fat: 7 Carbohydrates: 82 g Protein: 6 g Cholesterol: 0 mg Sodium: 319 mg

SALADS

Asian Noodle Steak Salad

Serve this salad warm or cold for a delicious, satisfying meal.

½ lb.	lean beef steak	¼ c.	low sodium soy sauce
1	red pepper, seeded and thinly sliced	1 t.	black pepper
		½ t.	ground ginger
1 c.	fresh bean sprouts	1	clove garlic, minced
8 oz.	vermicelli pasta, cooked and drained	1 t.	brown sugar
		½ t.	Asian chile oil
		3 oz.	dry roasted peanuts, coarsely chopped

Remove all visible fat from the beef. Cut the beef into very thin slices. Coat the grill with cooking spray and preheat for 5 minutes. Grill the beef for 3–5 minutes, or according to your preference. In a large serving bowl, combine the beef, red pepper, bean sprouts and pasta. In a small bowl, prepare the salad dressing by combining the soy sauce, black pepper, ginger, garlic, brown sugar and chile oil. Pour the dressing over the salad and toss all the ingredients together. Top with the chopped peanuts. Serves 6.

NUTRITIONAL ANALYSIS: Calories: 217 Total fat: 11 g Saturated fat: 2 g
% calories from fat: 43 Carbohydrates: 18 g Protein: 15 g Cholesterol: 23 mg Sodium: 708 mg

Garden Vegetable Fettuccini Salad

A colorful and flavorful lunch or dinner entrée.

1	red pepper, cut into 1-inch pieces	1 T.	roasted garlic flavored oil
1	green pepper, cut into 1-inch pieces	2 T.	balsamic vinegar
		1 t.	Italian seasoning
2 c.	eggplant, cut into ½ inch pieces	1 T.	fresh parsley, minced
½ c.	onion, cut into 1-inch pieces	½ t.	salt
1	clove garlic, finely minced	½ t.	dried rosemary
1	tomato, chopped	1 t.	coarsely ground black pepper
8 oz.	fettuccini noodles, cooked		nonfat cooking spray

Coat the grill with cooking spray and preheat for 5 minutes. Place the peppers, eggplant, onion and garlic in the grill and cook for 6–8 minutes. In a large serving bowl, combine the grilled vegetables, chopped tomato and fettuccini noodles. Mix together the oil, vinegar, Italian seasoning, parsley, salt, rosemary and black pepper to make the salad dressing. Pour the dressing over the salad and toss gently to blend the flavors. Serves 6.

NUTRITIONAL ANALYSIS: Calories: 93 Total fat: 3 g Saturated fat: >1 g % calories from fat: 26 Carbohydrates: 15 g Protein: 3 g Cholesterol: 12 mg Sodium: 14 mg

Summer Berry Salad

Pair this salad with Sage-Stuffed Chicken Breasts (p. 141),
for a perfect summer evening meal!

2 c.	strawberries, cleaned and cut in halves
1 c.	raspberries, cleaned
½ c.	fresh blueberries
1	peach, peeled, pitted and sliced
½ c.	nonfat sour cream
1 t.	sugar
1 T.	lemon juice

In a large salad bowl, combine the fruit. Mix together the sour cream, sugar and lemon juice in a small bowl and drizzle over the fruit. Toss lightly and serve at once. Serves 4.

NUTRITIONAL ANALYSIS: Calories: 89 Total fat: >1 g Saturated fat: >1 g
% calories from fat: 5 Carbohydrates: 20 g Protein: 3 g Cholesterol: 0 mg Sodium: 32 mg

Grilled Chicken Fruit Salad

Serve this as a light luncheon or supper entrée.

1	chicken breast half, skinned and boned
2 c.	seedless red grapes, halved
½ c.	celery, chopped
¼ c.	onion, chopped
2 T.	walnuts, finely chopped
½ c.	nonfat mayonnaise
1 T.	Dijon mustard
½ t.	salt
½ t.	black pepper
1 T.	lemon juice
	nonfat cooking spray

Lightly coat the grill with cooking spray and preheat for 5 minutes. Grill the chicken for 5–7 minutes. Cool and cut into small cubes. In a large salad bowl, combine the chicken, grapes, celery, onion and walnuts. Mix together the mayonnaise, mustard, salt, pepper and juice to make a dressing. Pour over the chicken salad and toss lightly. Serves 4.

NUTRITIONAL ANALYSIS: Calories: 222 Total fat: 5 g Saturated fat: >1 g
% calories from fat: 21 Carbohydrates: 24 g Protein: 15 g Cholesterol: 37 mg Sodium: 671 mg

Green Garden Salad with Herb & Bacon Vinaigrette

An appetizing salad to accompany almost any entrée.

4 c.	torn dark green lettuce leaves		2 T.	olive oil
½ c.	celery, sliced		2 T.	balsamic vinegar
4	radishes, sliced		2 T.	water
½ c.	frozen peas, thawed and drained		1 t.	garlic powder
1	large tomato, cut into wedges		½ t.	salt
½	small purple onion, sliced and separated into rings		1 t.	black pepper, coarsely ground
4	slices turkey bacon			nonstick cooking spray

In a large salad bowl, combine the lettuce, celery, radishes, peas, tomato and onion. Refrigerate. Lightly coat the grill with cooking spray and preheat for 5 minutes. Grill the bacon for 3–4 minutes. Cool, crumble and set aside.

Assemble the dressing by blending the oil, vinegar, water, garlic powder, salt and pepper. Shake well. Pour the dressing over the salad, toss the ingredients and garnish with the bacon. Serves 4.

NUTRITIONAL ANALYSIS: Calories: 195 Total fat: 9 g Saturated fat: 1 g
% calories from fat: 49 Carbohydrates: 16 g Protein: 6 g Cholesterol: 13 mg Sodium: 538 mg

Grilled Vegetable Pasta Salad

Fresh vegetables and tender pasta make a beautiful presentation!

2	zucchini, thinly sliced
1	small purple onion, thinly sliced
1	clove garlic, finely minced
1	red pepper, chopped
8 oz.	linguine, cooked
1 T.	balsamic vinegar
2 T.	olive oil
1 t.	black pepper
½ t.	oregano
2 T.	Italian parsley, chopped
½ t.	salt
1	tomato, chopped
	nonfat cooking spray

Coat the grill with cooking spray and preheat for 5 minutes. Place the zucchini, onion, garlic and red pepper in the grill and cook for 6–8 minutes. In a large serving bowl, combine the grilled vegetables and cooked linguine.

In a small bowl, combine the vinegar, oil, black pepper, oregano, Italian parsley and salt to make the dressing. Pour the dressing over the linguine and vegetables, toss and garnish with the chopped tomato. Serves 4.

NUTRITIONAL ANALYSIS: Calories: 172 Total fat: 8 g Saturated fat: 1 g
% calories from fat: 39 Carbohydrates: 22 g Protein: 5 g Cholesterol: 19 mg Sodium: 302 mg

CHAPTER 9

THE GEORGE FOREMAN LEAN MEAN FAT REDUCING GRILLING MACHINE BASIC COOKING GUIDE

To adapt your recipes to the *George Foreman Grilling Machine* and to create new ones, we suggest you start with the basic cooking guide that follows. Food is very rarely perfectly uniform in size; so you'll find that some of the suggested times will need to be adjusted to your foods as they grill. We've included the following tips that will help you enjoy the full range of features offered by your *George Foreman Grilling Machine*:

■ Carefully read the Owner's Manual that accompanies your grill. The grill is an easy and carefree appliance when used and cleaned properly.

■ If your grilling machine includes extension feet, use them as directed when you are preparing fillings for tacos or fajitas, or for mixtures containing rice. Use the plastic spatula to remove fillings from the grill and spoon directly into tortillas or onto individual plates.

■ Some foods cook more uniformly when placed horizontally or vertically in the grill. For example, asparagus should be placed lengthwise (vertically) across the grill. Most kebabs grill best widthwise (horizontally) across the grill. If you aren't sure which way is best, try one direction for about 1–2 minutes and then check the food. Rearrange food as needed.

- An uneven cut of meat or a chop may display "char marks" on one side as it grills. Although this does not have any effect on the results of the grilled foods, you may rearrange the meat to "even out" the marks, if you desire. You do not have to turn meat over while it grills because the grill cooks both sides at the same time, however you may turn meat if you want to baste it or reposition it.

- We suggest you use a nonfat cooking spray in the grill prior to putting foods into it. This is optional, but it helps to protect the nonstick grill surface and aids in removing the food after it grills.

The George Foreman Lean Machine
Fat Reducing Grilling Machine Basic Cooking Guide

Food	Grilling Minutes	Notes
Beef		
Flank steak	7–8	Slice thinly to serve
Hamburger, 4 oz.	7–8	
8 oz.	8–9	
Kebabs	7–8	1-inch pieces
London broil	7–8	1½–2 inches thick
Ribeye	5–7	
Ribs, Short ribs	8–9	Parboil prior to grilling
Loin ribs	7–8	Parboil prior to grilling
Round steak	5–7	
Sirloin	7–9	
T-Bone	8–9	
Tenderloin	5–7	
Fruit		
Apple	6–8	cut in half or sliced
Bananas	3–4	sliced lengthwise
Nectarines	3–5	cut in half or sliced
Peaches	3–5	cut in half or sliced
Pineapple	5–7	½-inch thick slices

Food	Grilling Minutes	Notes
Lamb		
Ground lamb	6–7	
Kebabs	7–8	1-inch pieces
Loin chops	4–6	
Pork		
Center cut chops	5–6	
Ground pork	7–8	
Ham	3–4	fully cooked, ½-inch thick slice
Kebabs	7–8	1-inch pieces
Loin chops	5–6	
Ribs, Baby back ribs	5–7	Parboil prior to grilling
Country-style ribs	8–10	boneless
Sausage	5–6	lowfat, link or patty style
Tenderloin	4–6	
Poultry		
Chicken breasts	5–7	boneless/skinless
Chicken kebabs	7–8	1-inch pieces
Chicken sausage	5–7	lowfat, link or patty style
Chicken thighs	5–7	boneless/skinless
Ground chicken	7–8	
Ground turkey	7–8	
Turkey breast, boneless/skinless		
Thin sliced	3–4	
Sliced	5–7	¼–½ inch thick

Food	Grilling Minutes	Notes
Sandwiches		
Cheese	6–7	
Ham	5–6	
Roast Beef	6–7	
Rueben	5–6	
Sausage	6–7	
Turkey	6–7	
Seafood		
Halibut steak	6–8	½–1 inch thick
Kebabs	4–6	1–inch pieces
Mahi Mahi fillet	3–5	
Orange Roughy fillet	4–6	
Red Snapper fillet	3–5	
Salmon, Fillet	3–4	
Steak	6–8	½–1 inch thick
Scallops	4–6	
Sea Bass fillet	3–5	
Shrimp	1½–2½	
Swordfish steak	6–9	½–1 inch thick
Tuna steak	6–8	½–1 inch thick
Snacks		
Calzone	8–9	
Hot Dogs	2–3	
Quesadillas	2–3	
Tacos	6–8	meat filling

Food	Grilling Minutes	Notes
Vegetables		
Asparagus	3–4	lengthwise (vertically) on grill
Brussels sprouts	8–9	frozen, thawed
Carrots	5–7	¼–½ inch thick slices
Eggplant	8–9	¼–½ inch thick slices or cubed
Onions	5–6	thinly sliced
Peppers	6–8	thinly sliced
Potatoes, Baking	7–9	¼–½ inch thick slices or cubed
Red	7–9	¼–½ inch thick slices or cubed
Sweet	7–9	¼–½ inch thick slices or cubed
Squash	6–8	¼–½ inch thick slices or cubed

Personal Notes

Food	Grilling Minutes	Notes

Personal Notes

Food	Grilling Minutes	Notes

Personal Notes

Food	Grilling Minutes	Notes

Personal Notes

Food	Grilling Minutes	Notes

GLOSSARY

Acid reaction. Marinades are typically based on ingredients that contain acids, such as vinegar or citrus juice. The meat reacts to the acid in the marinade, which breaks down the connective tissue of the meat and tenderizes it during the process.

Asian chile oil. A very spicy oil laced with chile peppers that can be found in the Oriental section of most grocery stores.

Balsamic vinegar. This flavored vinegar that has its roots in the balsam tree. Balsamic vinegar is especially popular as in ingredient in salad dressings and marinades.

Cajun. From the heart of Louisiana, the term "Cajun" is used to define a hot and spicy mixture of herbs and spices. Most commonly, the spices are used as rubs for blackened meat, poultry or fish and as seasonings in soups and stews.

Calorie. A unit measurement of an energy-producing value. Calories are present in almost all natural foods.

Carbohydrate. Compounds of carbon, hydrogen and oxygen. Found in foods that contain sugars (lactose, fructose, maltose, etc.) and/or starches.

Cayenne pepper. A condiment made from ground dried red peppers.

Chili powder. A combination of spices including cayenne pepper and garlic powder.

Cilantro. A parsley known for flat leaves and distinct flavor, cilantro is especially popular in Mexican foods. Used in salsas, marinades and sauces.

Coriander. This aromatic herb is from the carrot family.

Couli. A thick sauce that is used as a presentation as well as an accompaniment. Typically, a couli (or coulis) is spooned onto a plate and the entrée is placed on top of the couli.

Cumin. A traditional Mexican spice from the carrot family, cumin is used to add bold flavor to a variety of foods.

Dijon mustard. This mustard is distilled with white wine and spices. Dijon mustard is more smooth and mellow than the more common yellow mustard.

Fillet. A fillet refers to a piece of fish or meat that has been de-boned.

Gram. A metric unit, equivalent to .035 ounces, that is used to measure fat.

Hoisin sauce. A smooth, dark Oriental sauce that adds flavor to meat, poultry and fish. Found in the Oriental section of the grocery store or in specialty markets.

Kebab. A cubed piece of meat, fish, poultry, fruit or vegetable that is skewered prior to cooking.

Liquid smoke. Used to add barbeque flavoring, liquid smoke is available in the spice section of the grocery store.

Lowfat. A standardized term based on the U.S. Department of Agriculture ratings that refer to foods that have a proportionately low number of fat grams. Any commercially prepared food that claims to be "reduced fat, lowfat or nonfat" must meet these ratings to support the claim.

Marbled. This term is used to describe the amount of fat running through a cut of beef. Although the marbling in beef is what contributes to the flavor and tenderness, it is also a major contributor of fat.

Marinade. A brine (acid-based) sauce used to infuse flavor and tenderness in meat, fish, poultry and vegetables.

Mop. This popular term is used as a description for a thick barbeque and grilling sauce. Mops are also used as table sauces.

Nutrient. A substance or ingredient that nourishes or promotes health.

Papparelle. A curly-edged pasta found in specialty or gourmet food stores.

Parboil. To partially cook foods by the indirect method of steaming. Parboiling is recommended for ribs prior to grilling in the *George Foreman Grilling Machine.*

Pesto. A sauce based on the herb, basil, which is used to accompany a wide variety of Italian foods.

Rub. A combination of spices and herbs pressed into a cut of meat, poultry or fish directly prior to cooking.

Sage. A savory herb that belongs to the mint family. Sage has traditionally been used as an accompaniment to poultry.

Searing. The quick introduction of foods to high temperatures during the cooking process. Foods that sear on the exterior during grilling form a seal to preserve juices on the interior.

Sodium. The element term for salt.

Szechwan spicy sauce. The extra-hot Oriental sauce based on chile oil. Used sparingly, it creates the "heat" in Szechwan dishes. Found in the Oriental section of the grocery store.

Tamari. An aged soy sauce that is fermented longer than typical soy sauces for extra richness and flavor. Found in Oriental and specialty markets.

Turmeric. An East Indian herb from the ginger family. Commonly used in curry, turmeric (or tumeric, as it is sometimes spelled) can be found in the spice section of the grocery store.

Zest. The finely grated peel from fruit such as lemon or orange.

INDEX

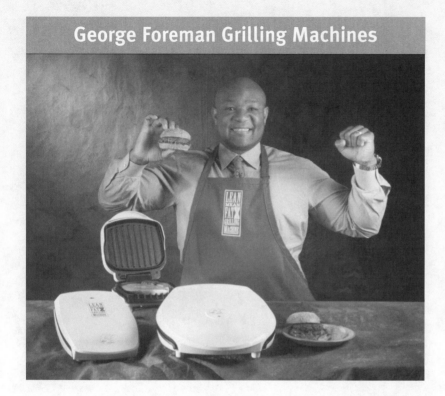

George Foreman Grilling Machines

LEAN MEAN FAT REDUCING GRILLING MACHINE

For information or to order any of these other products
in the George Foreman "family," call Salton at

1-800-233-9054

or visit our website:

http//www.salton-maxim.com

or e-mail us at Salton@Saltonusa.com

innovation for a healthier today and tomorrow